PIDGIN
PHRASEBOOK

Trevor Balzer
Ernie Lee
Peter Mülhäusler & Paul Monaghan

Denise Angelo
Dana Ober

Pidgin phrasebook
2nd edition – July 1999 (revised)

Published by
Lonely Planet Publications Pty Ltd ABN 36 005 607 983
90 Maribyrnong St, Footscray, Victoria 3011, Australia

Lonely Planet Offices
Australia Locked Bag 1, Footscray, Victoria 3011
USA 150 Linden St, Oakland CA 94607
UK 72-82 Rosebery Ave, London, EC1R 4RW
France 1 rue du Dahomey, 75011 Paris

Cover illustration
by Brendan Dempsey, based on an original illustration by Annie Wu,
My Own Private Melanesiens

ISBN 1 74104 597 5

text © Lonely Planet Publications Pty Ltd 1999
cover illustration © Lonely Planet Publications Pty Ltd 1999

9 8 7 6 5 4   2 1

Printed by the Bookmaker International Ltd
Printed in China

About the Authors

Trevor Balzer wrote the Bislama chapter. He lives on the Gold Coast in Queensland, Australia. Among the things he enjoys are spending times with friends, the solitude and beauty of the wilderness and the infrequent opportunities to get his mountain bike dirty. In 1980 Trevor first visited the Islands of Vanuatu. The people and the place were to have a profound and lasting impact on his life. Vanuatu is now a second home. Over the years Trevor has travelled to the archipelago on numerous occasions. At present Trevor is studying Bislama for his doctorate in Applied Linguistics, with an emphasis on the differences between urban and rural dialects of the language.

He would like to thank John Rutherford for his help proofreading the early draft of this document; Roly Sussex for his help with stylistics and presentation, and in particular for their marathon long distance phone call which proved crucial to the finished product; Ralph, Joel and Fiona for their assistance with local history and some of the finer points of Bislama grammar; Gary Williams and Brendon Teefy for letting him use their computers while his was 'at the doctors'. Finally, he would like to thank his many friends for their encouragement and support throughout the project.

When he first accepted the task of writing this chapter he had no idea how difficult and time consuming it would prove to be. It's not easy to formalise one's knowledge of a language. He trusts, however, that what he has provided will provide a sound foundation to build upon. Sometimes 'getting your feet wet' is the only way to really learn.

Dr Ernie Lee wrote the chapter on Solomon Islands Pijin. He and his wife Lois, both from the USA, have been living and working in the Solomon Islands since 1979 under the auspices of the Solomon Islands Christian Association. His PhD is in linguistics from Indiana University completed in 1966.

Ernie enjoys travelling and has been to many of the islands of the Solomon archipelago as part of his work. A favourite activity is walking and running in the Easter Fun Run in Honiara each year. He is recognised widely in the Solomons as the man with the white beard.

During the past 20 years, Ernie's work has included a program for developing Pijin as a written language, teaching Solomon Islanders to read and write Solomon Islands Pijin and advising on the translation of the New Testament of the Bible into Pijin. Currently he is teaching the principles of translation to the students at Bishop Patteson Theological College on Guadalcanal and helping them apply those principles by translating materials from English into Solomon Islands Pijin. One of the things that motivates him most is seeing students become excited about the potential of Pijin as a written language as well as an oral means of communication.

He would like to thank Hilda Kwanae and Conrad Manfort of the Pijin Old Testament Project for their contribution in writing the first drafts of the parts of this chapter related to food and culture. Thanks go also to the many different Solomon Islanders, especially his students, who have helped him learn Pijin during the 20 years he has lived in the Solomons. As his students well know he's still learning. Finally he would like to thank his wife Lois for her love, support, and encouragement.

Peter Mühlhäusler, one of the authors of the Tok Pisin chapter, lives in Aldgate, in the Adelaide Hills, South Australia. He is the Foundation Professor of Linguistics at the University of Adelaide and has spent many months doing fieldwork on the laguages of the Pacific and Australia. He completed his PhD thesis on Tok Pisin in 1976 but has published on this language ever since and occasionally offers language classes. In his spare time he enjoys working on his seven acre paradise, spending time modelling trains, interacting with his ferrets and bees and being with family and friends.

Paul Monaghan is the other author of the Tok Pisin Chapter. He is a postgraduate student at the University of Adelaide, where he has studied pidgin languages of the Australia-Pacific region. His interests are AFL (Australian Rules Football), reading and oysters.

Denise Angelo wrote the section on Kriol. She is the Senior Linguist for Diwurruwurru-jaru Aboriginal Corporation (the Katherine Regional Aboriginal Language Centre), which services over 30 traditional Aboriginal languages and the new Aboriginal language of the region, Kriol.

Denise Angelo would like to thank Maureen Hodgson who told the *Hunting with Billycans* story reproduced in this book; Annemarie Huddleston, provided many ideas and language idioms that assisted with the phrases section; Barbara Raymond who was of great assistance with providing insights into how the Kriol language works as a system; the great many Kriol speakers, especially sanrais-wei (to the east) at Ngukurr, Urapunga, Minyerri, Jilkminggan, Barunga, Beswick, Bulman and Katherine and also san-gu-dan-wei (to the west) over in Kununurra, who taught Denise about Kriol and talked to her in Kriol.

Dana Ober wrote the section on Yumpla Tok. Thanks to Anima Ghee, Bakoi Pilot and Puitam Wees for contributions on languages.

From the Publisher
Vicki Webb proofread and wrote the introduction, Olivier Breton edited, Brendan Dempsey laid out the text, Joanne Adams laid out the cover, Annie Wu did the beautiful cover art and the illustrations, Jim Miller supplied maps. Peter D'Onghia provided the pikininis with guidance (and betel nut) and Sally Steward made sure they behaved.

CONTENTS

Pidgin languages have arisen when people from different language backgrounds have come into frequent contact, through trade, on plantations, and on mission settlements. In their most basic form, pidgins are generally characterised by their use as a secondary language and by their regular and simplified grammars.

A pidgin may be creolised – that is, undergo a rapid expansion in vocabulary and grammar – when its speakers require a more sophisticated form of communication than was at first necessary. This can happen when children learn a pidgin as their first language, or when it becomes the main language of a community. (Creole languages are popularly known as pidgins. They are referred to as such here.)

Several pidgins have developed in the southwest Pacific and northern Australia, including Bislama (Vanuata), Pijin (Solomon Islands), Tok Pisin (Papua New Guinea), Yumpla Tok (Torres Strait Islands) and Kriol (northern Australia). These languages function as lingua francas (common languages), in some of the most diverse linguistic environments in the world.

English-based pidgins were once spoken on many of the islands throughout the Pacific, although most of these are no longer used. Some, such as Pacific Pidgin English, were spread by the traders, fishermen and plantation workers who used them. From the mid 1860s to the turn of the century, Solomon Islanders, ni-Vanuatu and other Pacific Islanders went to work, sometimes forcibly, on plantations in coastal Queensland. In this mixed language environment, a pidgin developed which formed the base of lingua francas in Vanuatu and the Solomon Islands when these workers returned to their respective islands. Similarly, labourers from New Guinea learned pidgin on Samoan plantations between 1880 and WWI, which they brought back to PNG and developed into one of the world's most widely spoken pidgins, Tok Pisin.

Various pidgins were also once spoken in Australia, mainly as a means of communication between Aboriginals and Europeans. Most of these died out when they were no longer needed, or merged to form one pidgin. In northern Australia, a widely spoken pidgin became the lingua franca of a Northern Territory mission settlement in the early 20th century, where speakers of several Aboriginal languages took refuge after being brutally driven off their land. And in the Torres Strait, to the north of Australia, a local pidgin developed when Pacific Islanders set up a fishing industry in the mid 19th century, bringing Pacific Pidgin with them.

Pacific and Australian pidgins have developed into distinct languages with their own vocabulary, grammar, and consonant and vowel systems. They are now used as a first language by some speakers, and are widely spoken within their communities. As they're based on English, some words may appear familiar. However, like any language, a pidgin can't be properly spoken or understood without some awareness of its structure as well as its vocabulary. Pidgins often reflect characteristics of the indigenous languages of their speakers. Pronunciation, especially when speakers have little exposure to English, can be similar to that of local languages, and words borrowed from English may have taken on new meanings. Grammatical influence can often be seen in, among other things, the differences in the pronoun systems of pidgins and English.

As with other languages, pidgins can vary from speaker to speaker. Some speakers pronounce words as they would sound in their indigenous language(s), while others model their pronunciation more closely on English. Many may vary their pronunciation depending on who they're speaking with. Words borrowed from indigenous languages used in pidgins may also vary from region to region.

Although attitudes toward pidgins in the past have often been negative, today they're recognised as valid languages which allow their speakers a full range of expression. They're used in a variety of contexts, such as the home, in the media, in education, and in government. Although developed from languages initally seen as temporary means of communication, the pidgins of Australia and the Pacific have now become an integral part of the identity of their speakers.

ABBREVIATIONS USED IN THIS BOOK

sg   singular
pl   plural

Bislama

BISLAMA

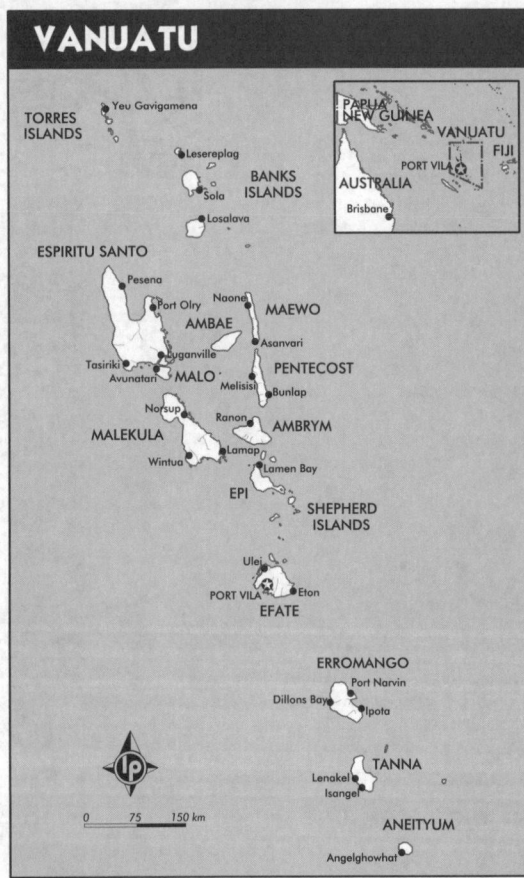

VANUATU

TORRES ISLANDS
Yeu Gavigamena

Lesereplag

BANKS ISLANDS
Sola
Losalava

ESPIRITU SANTO
Pesena
Port Olry   Naone
AMBAE   MAEWO
Luganville   Asanvari
Tasiriki   MALO   PENTECOST
Avunatari   Melisis Bunlap
Norsup   Ranon AMBRYM
MALEKULA
Wintua   Lamap   Lamen Bay
EPI
SHEPHERD ISLANDS

Ulei
PORT VILA   Eton
EFATE

ERROMANGO
Port Narvin
Dillons Bay   Ipota

TANNA
Lenakel
Isangel

ANEITYUM
Angelghowhat

0   75   150 km

PAPUA NEW GUINEA
VANUATU
PORT VILA   FIJI
AUSTRALIA
Brisbane

INTRODUCTION

Bislama is the English-based pidgin used in Vanuatu. Within a population of approximately 165,000, Vanuatu has over one hundred different languages. With an average of one language for every 1600 people, it is one of the most linguistically diverse regions anywhere in the world. A number of traditional languages are to some extent mutually intelligible, but Bislama is the only language which transcends all groups and serves as a common language.

While Bislama is widely used, not necessarily everyone speaks it. For many ni-Vanuatu (a term denoting local nationality), or ni-Vans as the people often refer to themselves, it is their second or even third language. A new generation of ni-Vans, however, is growing up with Bislama as their first language.

As a legacy of the former joint British and French colonial governments, both English and French are also used. When Vanuatu gained its independence in 1980, the newly formed government installed them as the nation's official languages. Relatively few locals, however, could speak either of these languages with first language fluency. English has by far the higher usage of the two, and some of the locals would be able to take part in simple conversations. An English speaking traveller would have little difficulty communicating in Port Vila, the nation's capital and main tourist area.

Bislama's economic, social and political importance to Vanuatu life is paramount. To the keen traveller, it offers the possibility of visiting almost any region in the archipelago.

It's not extremely difficult to acquire the basics of Bislama in a relatively short period of time.

History

Early forms of Bislama arose in the western Pacific during the 19th century as a simplified means of communication between islanders and European traders. The name 'Bislama' itself originally derives from the Portuguese *bicho do mar* meaning 'small sea creature'. It was known in French as *biche la mar*, meaning 'sea slug' (or 'trepang'). In the mid 1800s, a lucrative trade developed in the western Pacific for this Chinese delicacy. The pidgin that developed in these situations drew its name from the object of the trade.

The link between Bislama and the pidgins and jargons of the early to mid 1800s is unclear. The 1860s, however, saw the development of sugar-cane plantations in a number of areas, most notably in North Queensland (Australia). This development was to have a profound impact on Bislama.

Tropical North Queensland is typically hot and humid, conditions not at all favourable for European labourers, who felt much more at home in the cooler climate of the south. Pacific Islanders were a logical choice. They were well suited to the harsh conditions, and were known to be capable of hard work.

MISTAKEN IDENTITY

In 1606 the Portuguese explorer De Quirros discovered a land mass in the western Pacific so large, he thought it to be the long rumoured and much sought after great southern continent. He gave it the name *Terra Australis Del Espiritu Santo* 'the Great South Land of the Holy Spirit'. It took nearly 150 years to prove him wrong.

Today the island still retains a legacy of this early error in the name, *Espiritu Santo*, 'Holy Spirit' (the largest island in the Vanuatu archipelago). Ironically, in the very same year of De Quirros' discovery, the Dutchman Jansz became the first recorded European to actually walk on *Terra Australis Incognita* 'the unknown land in the south' when he made an inadvertent landfall on its northern coastline. Today, of course, it's simply called Australia.

Between the mid 1860s and the early 1900s, approximately 60,000 Pacific Islanders were transported to the sugar-cane plantations of Queensland. Many of them came from Vanuatu.

The methods used by the labour recruiters to fill their 'quota' of natives have been the topic of much debate over the years. The term 'blackbirding' often surfaces. It refers to the practice of abducting recruits and forcing them to work for plantation owners as slave labour. Many ni-Vanuatu will talk of how their ancestors were stolen. There is evidence, however, of both blackbirding and contract labour.

The multitude of languages converging on these locations created a situation where a common language was necessary if the workforce was going to be able to communicate, even at the most basic level. Plantation pidgins emerged in these situations as a blend of the various pidgins, jargons, European languages and local traditional languages that were spoken in or around the various plantations. Many of the South Sea Islander labour force would have arrived in Queensland already with some knowledge of broken English from earlier beach trade (such as trepang and sandalwood), or from serving as crew members on ships. The plantation pidgin that developed in Queensland became the earliest attested 'ancestor' of modern day Bislama.

The term 'Kanaka' was coined during this time to refer to the Pacific Islanders working on the plantations. The exact origins of the term are unclear, but one possible explanation is that 'Kanaka' was derived from the English 'cane hacker'.

The stability provided by 'long-termers' to plantation social life proved instrumental to the development of plantation pidgin, which became known as Queensland Kanaka Pidgin English. The newcomers learned from the old-guard.

By 1906 the practice of Islander labour was banned in Australia. When ni-Vanuatu recruits were returned, particularly from the late 1800s onwards, their pidgin language inevitably went with them, although a large number of the workers, settled in North Queensland.

BISLAMA

The new language found its place in Vanuatu life, mixing with the existing pidgins and jargons, local traditional languages and European languages, especially English. The result was a language unique to Vanuatu.

By and large, the sharing of 'Queensland Kanaka Pidgin English' with workers from other Pacific Island neighbours, such as Papua New Guinea, the Torres Strait, and in particular the Solomon Islands, is responsible for the relatively high degree of mutual intelligibility between the pidgins in this region. To be able to speak any of these pidgins would permit some communication with speakers of the other varieties. Different historical factors came into play in Papua New Guinea and the Torres Strait which, in part, account for some of the variation between these two and the present day pidgins of the Solomon Islands and Vanuatu.

WWII also had a significant impact on Bislama. Vanuatu, and in particular the Island of Espiritu Santo, were to become a US military base for the Coral Sea. The mass 'invasion' of English-speaking Americans to the region gave many ni-Vanuatu extensive exposure to Bislama's 'mother-language', for the first time.

PRONUNCIATION

Bislama often sounds extremely familiar to an English-speaking person. The apparent similarity of Bislama to English is largely due to the fact that around 85% of Bislama's vocabulary is derived from English.

The remainder of Bislama's vocabulary derives mainly from French, Portuguese, and from Melanesian and Polynesian languages. Bislama's vocabulary is far more restricted than English and totals between 4000 and 8000 words.

One thing that the observant visitor will inevitably notice is that there's a marked difference between Bislama as it's spoken in and around Port Vila, and the Bislama spoken in the villages. Town Bislama tends to be closer to English. The Bislama described in this section is more applicable to villages. It should be remembered that approximately 85% of the population live outside of Port Vila and the main towns.

There are a number of important things to know about Bislama's sound patterns. First, even though English words are used extensively, many English sounds are simplified such as 'sh' in 'show' and 'ch' as in 'church', which may not be heard in some varieties (this is changing). It is difficult to write these sounds as they are actually pronounced, they must be heard in order to be fully understood.

Vowels

i   as the 'e' in 'me'
e   as the 'e' in 'bet'
a   as the 'a' in 'afternoon'
u   as the 'oo' in 'good'
o   as the 'o' in 'hot'
ae   as the 'igh' in 'sight'
ea   as the 'ea' in 'clear', usually two sounds
oa   as the 'oo' in 'door', sometimes a single sound,
       sometimes two sounds as in 'boa'
ua   as the 'ore' 'shore', sometimes a single sound,
       sometimes two sounds
ao   as the 'ow' in 'town'
oe   as the 'oy' in 'boy'
ei   as the 'ay' in 'bay'

Consonants

Most consonants are similar in use and sound to English. A few exceptions are highlighted.

Remember that the lists here are generalisations and may not account for all regional variation, and that some of the sounds included are more peculiar to town Bislama.

g   as the 'g' in 'gang'
ng   as the 'ng' in 'gang'
ch   as the 'ch' in 'chop'

j   as the 'j' in 'juice' or 'ch' in 'chips'
y   as the 'y' in 'you'
r   as the 'r' in 'red', but the tip of the tongue raised

The following English consonants are often not distinguished in Bislama.

p and b   as in 'pat' and 'bat',
t and d   as in 'ted' and 'dead'
k and g   as in 'kit' and 'git'.

Following from this pig and pik are potentially the same word.

mb   has no true English equivalent, pronounced m + b
      (two sounds)
nd   has no true English equivalent, pronounced n + d
      (two sounds)

In Bislama you will hear mb, nd, and ng at the beginning of a syllable, as in mbae meaning 'will', 'would', 'could'. English sounds like ch has been included because they are becoming more common in town Bislama.

WRITTEN BISLAMA

Bislama developed as a spoken rather than as a written language. While this situation is changing, written Bislama is still far less prevalent. There are a few official publications in the language, including the Bible, and local newspapers which are printed in English, French and Bislama. Personal letters, of course, are often written in Bislama.

There is no official standard for writing Bislama. It is written the way it is spoken. Spelling tends to follow the principle of one sound equals one symbol. There may also be some regional variation.

Sometimes the Bislama way of writing does away with awkward and archaic English forms. For example, 'night' when borrowed into Bislama is written as naet. Also, in English, a single sound can be written in numerous ways. The simplicity of Bislama's system lets it be written only as ae. It is possible, though, to see a single word written in two or more different ways, even within a single text. The Bislama word for rubbish, doti (from 'dirty'), might also be written as toti. This may reflect a mixing of regional variations.

GRAMMAR

Bislama has its own distinct grammar. The use of traditional grammars during early stages of its development, to link foreign words, was instrumental in creating this situation.

Word Order

Bislama basically follows the subject-verb-object sequence similar to many languages, including English.

Verbs

There are three basic tenses in Bislama: past, present and future. There are no alterations of word form as in the English, 'to go', 'went', 'going' and 'gone'. In Bislama there's only one form of the verb, and tense is marked by the addition of special words.

Past Tense

Past events are marked with the addition of finis (from English 'finish') and/or bin (from English 'been'). Finis either directly follows the verb or comes at the end of the sentence.

---

i

i – a sound prevalent in Bislama, often appears as if it should be translated as 'is'.

Jon hem i stap   (lit: John he is here)

In reality it has no real English equivalent, so don't get hung up trying to force 'is' into every situation.

Similarly, it's quite difficult to give a literal translation for hemi, (hem + i) (see page 24). Where no literal translation is possible i has been listed as it appears in Bislama.

I've already eaten.   Mi kae kae finis.
I've eaten.   (lit: I eat finish)
I've finished eating.

I've already read the book.   Mi ridim buk ya finis.
I've read the book.   (lit: I read book this finish)
I've finished reading the book.

When there is no object after the verb, finis comes immediately
after. When the verb does have an object, finis appears after the
object.

Bin is used like the English 'has/have been'.

He's been working with me   Hem i bin wok wetem mi
  for five weeks now.   long faev wik finis.
                                    (lit: he/she been work with
                                    me for five week finish)

I've already been to town.   Mi bin long taon finis.
                                    (lit: I been to town finish)

Present Tense

The present tense is indicated with the addition of stap (from
English 'stop') or nothing at all. If stap is used, it's put immediately before the verb.

Where are you going?   Yu (stap) go we?
                                    (lit: you are go where)

I'm just going to town.   Mi (stap) go long taon
                                      nomo.
                                    (lit: I am go to town just)

Future Tense

To express the future add bae, mbae, or bambae (from English
'bye' and 'bye and bye'). Bae and mbae are interchangeable, and

tend to refer to an event in the immediate future. Bambae can be interchangeable (with bae or mbae), but it generally refers to an event in the more distant future. All three can be used to express the future, as in 'will' or 'shall', but bambae adds the notion of 'eventually'.

I'll see you later.	Bae/Mbae mi lukem yu.
	(lit: will I see you)
I'll see you around sometime.	Bambae mi lukem yu.
	(lit: eventually I see you)

Bae and mbae are more neutral and perhaps offer 'safer ground'. Also note that while bambae may be placed at the end of a sentence, bae and mbae may not. So, a sentence like Mi lukem yu bae (lit: I see you will) is *not* correct.

Transitive Verbs

Bislama verbs that are followed by an object will normally end in em, im or um.

open	openem : Mi openem buk ya.
	(lit: I open book this)
read	ridim : Mi ridim buk ya.
	(lit: I read book this)
push	pusum : Yu save pusum truk?
	(lit: you can push truck)

If the preceding vowel is e , -em is added. If it is i , -im is added. If it is u , -um is added. If the preceding vowel is not e, i, or u then -em is generally used. In this way wok (from English 'work') becomes wokem

Intransitive Verbs

Bislama verbs that aren't followed by an object (intransitive) do not end in -em, -im or -um.

leave	lego	(from English 'let go')
agree	agri	
learn	lan	

Some verbs may have both a transitive (with an object) and intransitive (without an object) form, an example being the verb lan (to learn).

| It's good if you learn English. | I gud sapos yu lanem Inglis. (lit: i good suppose you learn English) |
| It's good to learn. | I gud sapos yu lan. (lit: i good suppose you learn) |

Articles

Bislama doesn't have real equivalents to the English articles 'a' and 'the'. If you want to make a noun indefinite (a dog) or definite (the dog), it can be done by using, or not using, words like wan (from 'one'), wanfala (from 'one fellow'), sam (from 'some'), samfala (from 'some fellows'). Definiteness can also be shown by using ya meaning 'this', 'this one here'.

A girl spoke to me.	Wan gel hem i tok tok long mi. (lit: one girl she spoke to me)
The girl spoke to me.	Gel ya hem i tok tok long mi. (lit: girl this she spoke to me)
Some boys are going to town.	Samfala boe oli stap go long taon. (lit: some boy they are go to town)
The boys are going to town.	Olgeta boe oli stap go long taon. (lit: all boy they are go to town)

Nouns

Bislama nouns function in a similar way to English. There are
a few differences in their actual forms.

Plurality in Bislama is not marked by endings on words as with
's' in English. Nor are there forms like 'men' as a plural of 'man',
or 'mice' as the plural of 'mouse'. The noun form in Bislama
remains the same, regardless of how many items there might be.
Basic plurals are indicated by adding words such as tufala 'two' or
fulap 'many' as well as sam, samfala and olgeta (see page 22).

There are just two cars here.	Tufala truk nomo i stap. (lit: two car just i here)
There are many cars here.	Fulap truk i stap. (lit: full up car i here)

BISLAMA

INCLUSIVE & EXCLUSIVE LANGUAGE

An important thing to remember is that you have to
decide if you want to include the person(s) you are
talking to, or exclude them. If you get it wrong, you
won't be conveying the intended information. You may
even run the risk of offending by excluding someone
from an activity.

If you intend the person(s) you are addressing to
be included in an activity like going to the beach,
you should say:

Mbae yumi go long san bij long sava.	(lit: will we go to sand beach in afternoon) We are going to the beach this afternoon.

If you say:

Mbae mifala i go long san bij long sava.	(lit: will we go to sand beach in afternoon) We are going to the beach this afternoon.

you have excluded them from the activity.

Pronouns

Pronouns in Bislama are quite different from English. First, there are no special words for 'he', 'she' or 'it', (or 'him', 'her' or 'it'). On the other hand, Bislama is much richer than English when expressing number. While English only has singular (one) and plural (more than one), Bislama has a form for one, two, three and more than three. Bislama also has pronouns that can either include or exclude the person(s) being spoken to.

In Bislama, 'he', 'she', 'it', 'him', and 'her' are all expressed by hem:

He's from Pentecost Island.	Hem i man Pentekos. (lit: he man/person Pentecost)
She's a teacher.	Hem i wan tij. (lit: she one teacher)
It's very hot.	Hem i hot tumas. (lit: it hot very)

Relative Pronouns

We can be translated as 'that', 'who' 'which', 'where', according to context. Se, however, is more safely translated as 'that' when it precedes an expressed proposition.

I saw a man who was very old.	Mi lukem wan man we hem i olfala tumas. (lit: I saw one man that he old very)
I'm reading the book that you've been talking about.	Mi stap ridim buk we yu bin store long hem. (lit: I am read[ing] book that you been talking about it)
I said, 'Where are you going?'	Mi talem se, 'Yu stap go we?' (lit: I said that, 'you are go[ing] where')

I think it will be okay.	Mi ting se bae i olraet.
	(lit: I think that will i all right)
I hope you can come.	Mi hop se yu save kam.
	(lit: I hope that you can come)

BISLAMA

Singular

1st person	I	mi
2nd person	you	yu
3rd person	he/she/it	hem i

Plural

1st person exclusive

we (two)	mitufala i
we (three)	mitrifala i
we (more than three)	mifala i

1st person inclusive

we (two)	yumitu; yumitufala i
we (two)	yumitri; yumitrifala i
we (more than three)	yumi; yumi i; yumi evriwan

2nd person

you (two)	yutufala i
you (three)	yutrifala i
you (more than three)	yufala i

3rd person

they/them (two)	tufala i
they/them (three)	trifala i
they/them (more than 3)	olgeta i/olgeta/oli

Prepositions

One of the more common prepositions in Bislama is long. It can be translated as 'in', 'at', 'on', 'to' or 'by'.

He's in the car.
Hem i stap long truk.
(lit: he i in car)

I saw her at the shop.
Mi lukem hem long stoa.
(lit: I saw her at store)

It's on the table.
Hem i stap long tebol.
(lit: it i on table)

I have already been to town.
Mi bin long taon finis.
(lit: I been to town finish)

BISLAMA

Another preposition which is commonly used is blong or its shortened pronunciation blo. It has four uses in Bislama.

Possession

| This is my house. | Hem ya haos blong mi.
(lit: this house belonging me) |

Purpose

| I came to talk to you. | Mi kam blo tok tok long yu.
(lit: I came for the purpose of talk[ing] to you) |
| This a passenger ship. | Hem ya sip blong karem pasenja.
(lit: this ship is for the purpose of carrying passengers) |

Place of Origin

| Are you from this area? | Yu blong ples ya?
(lit: you belong/of place here) |
| I come from Australia. | Mi blo Ostrelia.
(lit: I belong/of Australia) |

Benefit

| He will finish this for me. | Mbae hemi finisim samting ya blong mi.
(lit: will he/she finish thing this for me) |
| I can do it for you. | Mi save mekem samting ya blo yu.
(lit: I can make/do thing this for you) |

BISLAMA

Other prepositions include wetem (from English 'with'), antap (from English 'on top'), and aninit (from English 'underneath').

He arrived with a football team.	Hemi kam wetem wan futbol tim.
	(lit: he came with one/a football team)
It's on top of the table.	Hem i stap antap long tebol.
	(lit: it is on top [of] table)
He's working under the car.	Hem i stap wok aninit long truk.
	(lit: he is work[ing] under car)

Conjunctions

The main conjunctions are mo 'and' (from English 'more'), o 'or' (from English 'or') and be 'but', 'although', 'however' (from English 'but').

Do you want tea or coffee?	Yu wantem ti o kofe?
	(lit: you want tea or coffee)
I'm not sure, but I think so.	Mi no sua, be mi ting olsem.
	(lit: I no sure, but I think like this)
I saw John and Mark at the market.	Mi lukem Jon mo Mak long maket.
	(lit: I saw John and Mark at market)

MORE, MORE, MORE

Both mo and moa derive from the English 'more' and share a similar pronunciation. When writing Bislama, however, mo is used to represent the conjunction 'and' whereas moa is often used to mean 'more'. The sentence Go moa lelebet (lit: go more little bit) wouldn't normally be written Go mo lelebet

BISLAMA

Questions

As in English, questions in Bislama often have a rising intonation on the last syllable.

- Questions that ask 'will' and 'shall' as in 'Will you come?' are formed by placing bae or mbae on the front of the sentence.

Will you come?   Mbae yu kam?
(lit: will you come)

Shall I finish this now?   Bae mi finisim samting ya noa?
(lit: shall I finish thing this now)

- Questions that ask 'can' or 'could', as in 'Can you come?' are formed by placing save after the subject.

Can you come?   Yu save kam?
(lit: you can come)

Could you come here?   Yu save kam long ples ya?
(lit: you can come to place here)

- Questions that ask 'when' wot taem, or 'where' we, have an inverted sentence order to English, with the 'wh' word going towards the end of the sentence.

Where are you going?   Yu stap go we?
(lit: you are going where)

When did you come?   Yu kam wot taem?
(lit: you came what time)

- Questions that ask 'why', from wanem (lit: because what), may or may not have an inverted sentence order to English.

Why did you do that?
    Yu mekem samting ia from wanem?/From wanem
    yu makem samting ia?
    (lit: you make thing this because what/because what
    you make thing this)

BISLAMA

- Questions that begin with 'is' can be formed in Bislama by using hemi immediately after the subject.

Is Trevor here?	Treva hemi stap? (lit: Trevor he i here)
Is Mark coming?	Mak i kam? (lit: Mark i coming)

- Hemi or i by themselves (without the subject) is OK if the subject is understood from the context of the conversation.

Is he/she/it coming?	Hemi kam? (lit: he/she/it i coming)
It is good?	I gud? (lit: i good)

Sometimes in Bislama, rising or falling intonation can be the only difference between a question and a statement. For example a conversation could go like this:

I gud? [rising intonation]	(lit: i good) Are you good?; How are you?
I gud. [falling intonation]	(lit: i good) I'm good.

BISLAMA

GOODNIGHT

Gud naet, doesn't necessarily mean that you're taking leave of the person immediately before going to sleep. While it can be used in this role, it's also widely used as a greeting from late afternoon/dusk, onwards. The locals will usually reply in kind if they haven't been the first to speak. Sometimes they might reply with a gentle raising of head and/or eyebrows. It can be subtle and is often missed by the outsider. This gesture can also be used to answer a question in the affirmative (yes).

MEETING PEOPLE

Ni-Vans are generally very sociable people. The locals tend to greet, or at least acknowledge (verbally or with body language) people they pass in the street or along a jungle track. It's good etiquette to reply in kind, and even to initiate the greeting, once you're familiar with procedures.

Greetings & Civilities

To greet someone who is far away, acknowledge them by raising your hand above your head. A loud halo (from English 'hello') may be appropriate if you are close enough.

If passing close to someone and you don't necessarily know them, these greetings can be used.

BISLAMA

Hello.	Halo.
Hello. (two people)	Halo tufala.
Hello. (three people)	Halo trifala/olgeta.
	(from English 'all together')
Hello. (more than three)	Halo olgeta.
Good morning.	Gud morning.
Good afternoon.	Gud aftenun.
Good night.	Gud naet.

If passing close to a person you know, Gud morning and Gud naet still apply, but a handshake and asking after the person's well-being may also be appropriate.

How are you?	Olsem wanem (long yu)?
How are you today?	Olsem wanem long yu tede ya?
Where are you going?	Yu go we?
Where did come from?	Yu kam we?

They may reply:

I'm OK; No worries.	Mi/i gud (nomo); I olraet (nomo).

BISLAMA

I am going to …	Mi stap go long …
town	taon
market	maket

I've come from …	Mi kam long …
the wharf	wof
Pangi (a village)	Pangi

DEGREES OF POLITENESS

As in English, Bislama has varying ways of making requests which determine politeness. In English, we use formulas like 'Could you …', 'Would you …', 'Please could you …', or even 'If it's possible/OK could you …'. It's much the same in Bislama.

The main words which can be added to show politeness are plis 'please', save 'can', mbae 'would', 'could', sapos i olraet;gud 'If it's OK/good'.

Would you come here please?	Plis mbae yu kam long ples ya?
Can you pass me the bread?	Yu save pasem bred i kam?
If it's okay could you …?	Sapos i olraet, yu save …?
take us to town	sakem mifala long taon
give me that book	givim buk ya long mi

Mbae is used here as 'could', 'would' or 'will' to soften a request. It can also be used to mark the future (see page 18).

Save, borrowed from English, but originally from the French savez, translates as 'can' or 'could' here. But it can also translate as 'knowledge' as in:

Mi no save.	I don't know.

If you don't want to say where you're going or where you've come from, it's OK to say something like:

No, mi wokbaot nomo.   I'm just going for a walk.

While in an urban area it might be unusual to stop, shake hands and start a conversation with someone you don't know, this is usually acceptable in the bush or while walking along a jungle path.

GOODBYES

Tata.	Goodbye.
Mi mas lego yu nao.	I must leave you (sg) now.
Mbae mi lego yufala noa.	I will leave you (more than three) now.
Mi mas go noa.	I must go now.
Mbae mi lukem yutufala.	I'll see you (two) around.
Mbae mi Lukem yu.	I'll see you later.
Lukem yu long nekis wik.	Catch you next week.

A full parting might go something like:

Ale! Mi mas go noa. Mbae mi lukem yu bakegen.
OK! I have to go now. I'll see you later.

The answer might be:

Ale!; Ale! I gud.
    OK! That's fine; No worries; Not a problem.

BISLAMA

Gratitude

Thank you.	Tangkiu/Tangkyu/Ta.

It's generally considered polite to add tumas, 'very much' (lit: too much) to expressions of gratitude.

Thank you very much.	Tangkiu tumas.
Thank you very much for …	Tangkiu tumas from …
the ice cream	aes krim
helping me/us	we yu givhan long mi/mifala

BISLAMA

OLD FELLOW

The term olfala (from English 'old fellow') is an acceptable form of address for an old man. If you know his name it's a good idea to include it while talking with him as in:

Halo olfala Mak.   Hello old fellow Mark.

If you suspect or know that he is a chief in his village, it's more appropriate to refer to him as jif. If in any doubt, it's better to simply say 'Hello' and ask for their name (see page 35). Take note and respond accordingly. This will enable you to address him in his preferred manner.

Language Difficulties

Here are a few phrases that might get you out of a tight spot:

Could you please repeat that?	Yu traem talem bakegen.
Could you say that again more slowly?	Yu traem talem bakegen slo lelebet?
I'm sorry but I don't understand (Bislama yet).	Sore, be me no save (Bislama yet).
I'm sorry but I only understand a little bit of Bislama.	Sore, be mi no save tumas Bislama yet.
Do you speak English?	Yu save tok tok long Inglis?
Do you understand English?	Yu save Inglis?
Is there anyone here who understands English?	I gat samwan long ples ya wi save Inglis?
How do you say ... in Bislama?	Olsem wanem yu save talem ... long Bislama?
Is ... the correct way of saying ... in Bislama?	... i stret blong talem ... long Bislama?

First Encounters

What's your name?	Wanem nem blong yu?
My name is …	Nem blong mi …
Trevor	Treva
Lyle	Lael
This is my first time in Vanuatu.	Hemi fas taem blong mi long Vanuatu.
I've been to Vanuatu before.	Mi bin long Vanuatu bifo.
I really like Vanuatu.	Mi laekem Vanuatu tumas.
How long have you been in (Vila)?	Yu bin stap long (Vila) hamas yia nao?
What island do you come from?	Yu blong wanem aeland?
Let's go for a walk.	(Ale) Yumi go wokbaot?
I'm/we're going for a walk.	Mi; Mifala i go wokbaot.

Family

How many children do you have?	Yu gat hamas pikinini?
What is/are your child(ren)'s name(s)?	Wanem nem blong (ol) pikinini blong yu?
How old is/are your child(ren)?	(Ol) pikinini blong yu i gat hamas yia?
I'm married.	Mi mared finis.

BISLAMA

TAKE THE TIME

Ni-Vans are great conversationalists and really enjoy anyone who will take time to talk. Local terms for conversation are store or store yarn (from 'story' and 'yarn'). To be known as Man blong store yarn 'a person who is good at the art of conversation' is a mark of distinction. Photographs from home can be a great conversation initiator.

BISLAMA

Age

How old are you?	Yu gat hamas yia?
I'm … years old.	Mi gat … yia finis.

Nationalities

You'll find that many country names in Bislama are very similar to English. If your country is not listed below try saying it in English and you'll most likely be understood.

I/we (exclusive) come from …   Mi/Mifala kam long …
    Australia   Ostrelia
    America   Amerika

USE AMONGST FRIENDS

Yu yes.   You're really something else.

Be careful how you use this one. It can be seen as a 'come on' depending on the situation.

Yu no makas.   You're good. (lit: you not rubbish)

Makas is 'rubbish' or a part of something that's normally discarded such as a banana peel or a coconut husk. This phrase can also be used in the sense of 'you're good value' or 'you really know what you're doing'.

Yu gud blong sop nomo.
    You're only good for making soap.

This is a humorous dig suggesting that someone's of little value. Use this with good friends only.

GETTING AROUND

In the major urban centres, especially Port Vila, there's no shortage of public transport. Small commuter buses and taxis run frequently. A short wait will generally get you a lift.

While there are official bus stops, it's normally possible to hail one almost anywhere. Buses don't have set routes, and you can direct your driver to close proximity of where you want to go. There's one standard fare for wherever you're going within the Port Vila municipal area.

If you want to venture outside town, you'll need to ask the price. Most taxi and bus drivers speak enough English to be able to understand your directions, but if you want to try out your Bislama or are trying to negotiate a taxi truck ride in one of the outlying islands or regions.

Useful Phrases

I want to go to the market/ post office.	Mi wantem go long maket/ postofis.
Can you wait for us?	Yu save wet long mifala?
Can you wait for a little while?	Yu save wet smol?
Can you come back at …?	Yu save kam bak long …?
noon	medel dei
quarter to six	fiftin minit i ronem siks
How much to take us to …?	Hamas blong go long …?
Takara (restaurant)	Takara
Havanah Harbour	Havana
Is that a return price?	Praes ya i gokam?
Will a bus/taxi come along this road?	Mbae bas/taksi i pas long rod ya?
Can I catch a bus from here?	Mi save singaot bas long ples ya?
Just go a little bit further.	Go moa lelebet.

Directions

Turn right here.	Tan raet long ples ya.
Turn left here.	Tan lef long ples ya.
Go up the hill.	Go antap.
Pull over here.	Stap long ples ya nomo.

BISLAMA

ACCOMMODATION

There are numerous accommodation options around Vanuatu, ranging from resort style to bungalows. Most travellers pre-arrange their booking before arriving, although it's possible to organise your requirements once in Vanuatu. Communicating your needs shouldn't be difficult, although a few basic phrases in Bislama may be useful, particularly in some of the more isolated locations.

Finding a Place

Some locals may not understand 'bungalow' or 'motel' so they are translated here as ples we turis i save slip, 'place where tourists can sleep'.

Is there a place I/we can stay close by?	I gat ples we i klosap we mi/mifala i save slip?
Where's a bungalow/motel?	Ples we turis i save slip i stap we?
I'm looking for a …	Mi stap lukaot wan ples we mi save slip we hemi …
place to stay	no dia/sas tumas
cheap	
clean	klin
good	gud wan
nearby	klosap nomo
near the town	klosap long taon
near the airport	klosap long efil

Checking In

Do you have any rooms/beds?	I gat rum/bed i stap?
I/we want a …	Mi/Mifala i wantem …
room for one/two/three/four	rum blong wan/tu/tri/fo
room with a double bed	rum wetem bed blong tu
large room	rum we i bigfala
small room	rum we i smolfala
How much it is per night?	Hamas long wan naet?
Is there a discount for two/three people?	I gat spesel praes long tu/tri pipol?

Is there a discount for children?	I gat spesel praes blong pikinini?
Is there a discount if I stay longer?	I gat spesel praes sapos mi stap long taem lelebet.
Can I see the room first?	Mi save lukem rum fastaem?
Can I have a look at another one?	Mi save lukem narawan bakegen?
This room will be fine.	Rum ya i gud.
I'm just going to stay for ...	Mbae mi stap ...
one/two nights	wan/tu naet nomo
two or three days	tu o tri dei nomo
one week	wan wik
Can I have a key please?	Yu save givim mi ki plis?
Any messages for me?	I gat mesej blong mi stap?
It's too ...	Hemi ... tumas
big/small	big/smol
hot/cold	hot/kol
dirty	doti

BISLAMA

Checking Out

I'll be leaving tomorrow.	Mbae mi livim yu tumora.
Can I pay my bill please?	Mi save pem kaon blong mi?
Thank you for your hospitality to (me/us).	Tangkiu tumas from we yu bin lukaot gud long mi/mifala.

Returning

I'll return ...	Mbae mi kambak ...
tomorrow	tumora
in two or three days	long tu o tri dei nomo
next week	long nekis wik

Once you've established some contacts, you might be able to arrange to stay in a village for a couple of nights. In this situation, never make it look like you're directly paying for your lodging. It's more appropriate to offer a gift (if possible from your home country) to your host family.

BISLAMA

FOOD

The Pidgin word (common across Melanesia) for food is kae or kae kae. As well as functioning as a noun, kae kae also serves as the verb 'to eat'. Furthermore, kae kae is also the name given to a traditional feast.

Western-type food can be purchased at stores and supermarkets. More traditional fare comes the garden, or is purchased from the market. Cooking is done either using saucepans and pots, or by the traditional hot stone method. The latter is a true culinary and aromatic delight.

Traditional Food

Lap Lap a thick, pudding-like meal prepared by the hot stone method. It can be made from a number of things, including taro, yam, maniok and banana. It's usually cooked and served wrapped in leaves.

Taro a large root-plant. Taro is easily recognised by its large elephant ear-like leaves growing above the ground. The best taro is usually grown underwater or in very damp ground. It's not uncommon to see creeks and streams diverted to irrigate gardens. Taro can be cooked in similar ways to potatoes.

Yam a small root-plant very similar to a potato or sweet potato

Maniok a small root-plant with a high starch content (also called 'cassava' and 'tapioca')

Kokonas krab 'coconut crab' is one of the true culinary delights in Vanuatu. It's a large land-based crab so named because coconut is the main item on its diet. Nowadays the kokonas krab is relatively rare, making it a fairly expensive item on the menu.

Bredfrut 'breadfruit' is the common name for the fruit of the moraceous tree. It's so named because when roasted it provides an acceptable substitute for bread.

Kava common in many regions in the Pacific, is the narcotic drink prepared by crushing the roots of the Kava plant. It's also possible to purchase a pre-packaged variety in local stores. You might be able to get a stronger version if you talk to some of the locals. A small taste will leave you with the 'just been to the dentist' feeling.

Other items on the local menu include raes 'rice', banana, popo 'paw paw/papaya', fis 'fish', flaenfokis 'fruit bat, flying fox', buluk 'beef', faol/jikin 'chicken' and pig 'pork'.

Western Food
Many Western 'fast food' items are available (especially in Port Vila).

hamburger	hambega
chips	jips
hamburger and chips	hambega jips
chicken and chips	jiken jips
ice cream	aes krim

The generic term for most juices and soft drinks (soda) is jus 'juice'. Koka (cola) is often distinguished from jus.

Useful Phrases

Can I try some of this?	Mi save traem smol long hem?
That smells beautiful.	Hemi smel naes.
The food is excellent.	Kae kae ya i numbawan.
I like this.	Hem i gud.
This is nicer than the other one.	Hemi winem narawan.
I'm full.	Mi fulap tumas; Hemi winim mi.
I can't eat another thing.	Mi no save kae kae wan samting bakegen.
Thank you so much for the lovely meal.	Tangkiu tumus from gudfala kae kae.
Thank you for all your hard work.	Tangkiu tumus from ol had wok blong yu.

Did you cook this in the hot stones?	Yu kukem samting ya long hot ston?
Do you have a garden?	Yu gat garen?
Where is your garden?	Garen blong yu i stap we?
What do you grow in your garden?	Yu gru wanem long garen blong yu?
Could I see your garden?	Mi save lukem garen blong yu?

SHOPPING

Saturday is the main market day in Port Vila (along the waterfront in the main shopping area). Local foods and crafts are set out for sale. It's usually a very colourful event and an excellent way of getting a taste of local culture. Smaller displays are often set up along a number of the side streets.

There's also a variety of shops, ranging from duty free stores and supermarkets to dealers of island artefacts. While Port Vila offers the most variety, other centres like Luganville (Espiritu Santo) have similar stores and markets.

In the rural areas, small co-op stores offer the basics, such as pre-packaged food items, drinks (usually non-refrigerated), toiletries and clothing.

Vatu is the local currency. Most, if not all, things will be quoted in this unit. Some outlets, however, will accept foreign money at the equivalent rate. Make sure to check the daily exchange rate. It's advisable to exchange your currency before arriving.

KOK IS IT

Don't use the term kok for 'cola drink', 'Coke' or 'Pepsi'. It can be mistaken for a vulgar expression. If you are unsure of what is meant, try pronouncing it to yourself. Terms like tin kok 'tin of Coke', botel kok 'bottle of Coke', or koka can be used to avoid any possible inappropriateness.

BISLAMA

Useful Phrases

What's this?	Wanem ya?
How much?	Hamas?
Do you have any more?	I gat mo i stap?
Do you have it in other colours?	I gat long nara kala bakegen?
This one's too big/small for me.	Hemi big wan; smol tumas long mi.
Do you have other sizes?	I gat nara saes bakegen?
How much for (one)?	Hamas long (wan)?
Did you make this?	Yu mekem samting ya?
Where did this come from?	Hemi kam long we?

Is ... money okay?	Mane blong ... i olraet?
Australian	Ostrelia
New Zealand	Niu Zilan
US	Amerika

How much is that in (Australian) currency? Hemi hamas long dola blong (Ostrelia)?

BARGAINING

Negotiating prices, or bartering, is not a generally accepted practice in Vanuatu. Everything normally has its Stret praes blong hem, 'set price'. If you think the price is too high, just say:

No thank you. No! I olraet tangyu tumas.

That's very expensive. Hemi dea tumas; Hemi sas tumas.

If you really want the item, come back later in the morning or afternoon – you might find the item at a lower price.

FESTIVALS & CELEBRATIONS

During the last week of July each year, culminating on the 30th, the people of Vanuatu selebretem Independens blong ol 'celebrate their Independence'. While smaller ceremonies are organised around many regional centres, the largest and most elaborate celebration takes place in Port Vila. Apart from the more formal aspects of the various programmes, numerous other activities such as sporting tournaments, are organised.

It's important to have some understanding of Vanuatu's struggle for freedom from colonial rule. From as early as the second half of the 19th century, both the British and the French were struggling for power in the archipelago. Neither really gained the upper hand, and in 1907, the ultimate political compromise was set up – a condominium (joint rule). For more than 70 years, the ni-Vanuatu lived under two political systems, incorporating two police systems, two jail systems, two schooling systems, two official languages, and the list goes on. The ni-Vanuatu received little benefit from the condominium. The terms 'farce' and 'pandemonium' were often used to refer to the awkward situations that developed.

Although the first major murmurs of independence surfaced in 1960s, self-rule eventually became a reality on 30th July 1980. Bislama was to play a significant role in this process. If the ni-Vanuatu were to present a unified front, they would need a common language. Bislama provided a means for people to come together. It enabled people of diverse language backgrounds to present a single voice in their struggle for freedom and ultimately to talk of themselves as Man Vanuatu, or Man blong Vanuatu 'a person belonging to Vanuatu'.

Two publications that will give the interested reader a deeper appreciation of this particular era in Vanuatu's history are *New Hebrides - The Road to*

BISLAMA

Independence edited by Chris Plant, University of the South Pacific, and *Beyond Pandemonium – From the New Hebrides to Vanuatu* by Father Walter Lini, Asia Pacific Research Unit. Both books should be fairly readily available in Port Vila.

A full-year diary of special events in Vanuatu can be located on the Web at <http://www.vanuatu.net.vu/pages/Vanuatu.html>

BISLAMA

NAGOL

One well known local mythological story recounts the legendary trickery of the wife of Tamale (Pentecost Island) who lured her husband into a tall tree and convinced him to commit suicide with her. They jumped. He fell to his death but she had secretly tied vines around her ankles, breaking her fall. Each year during the months of May and June the jump is re-enacted as men dive from constructed platforms as high as 35 metres with yam vines secured around their ankles. While the women are present, they aren't permitted to participate in the actual jump. The traditional name for the event is Nagol (the language of South Pentecost), although it is more commonly known simply as the Pentecost Jump or the Land Divers of Pentecost.

TRADITIONAL VANUATU

While significantly influenced by Western ways and values, Vanuatu has its own unique and rich cultures. Under colonialism, however, much of traditional Vanuatu was suppressed. In more recent years there's been a marked interest in its resurgence.

Aspects of life are generally considered:

fasin blong waetman	in the ways of the white man (lit: fashion of the white man)
fasin blong blakman	local custom (lit: fashion of the black man)

Alternate expressions for fasin blong blakman include:

> fasin blong man ples   (lit: ways of the people from
> this place)
>
> hemi blong man ples/   (lit: it belongs to people from
> Vanuatu   this place/it belongs to
> people of Vanuatu).

Quite often the simplified term kastom 'custom' is used by itself, as in kastom meresin 'traditional medicine'.

Custom in Vanuatu is bound more to the traditional languages than to Bislama. For every indigenous language there is a unique culture and mythology. While Bislama can be used to talk about traditional Vanuatu, it can't fully convey its richness. Phrases like fasin blong blakman are broad generalisations that only begin to capture the situation.

Although the ni-Vanuatu guard their traditional beliefs strongly, you'll find that with trust, comes an increasing willingness to share.

Useful Phrases

Do you have any traditional stories about this place?	Yufala i gat kastom store blong ples ia?
Are you able to tell me the story?	Yu save talem mi store blong hem?
I'd like to know more.	Mi wantem save moa.
Can I visit this cultural site?	Mi save go long kastom ples ia?
Can you take me to this place?	Yu save tekem me i go long ples ia?
May I take a photograph?	Mi save karem foto?
What things should I do?	Wanem ol samting i gud sapos mi mekem?
What things shouldn't I do?	Wanem ol samting i no gud sapos mi mekem?
Will you tell me if I do something wrong?	Mbae yu talem mi sapos mi mekem wan samting we i no stret?

BISLAMA

BISLAMA

Are there any places I shouldn't go?	I gat sam ples we i no gud sapos mi go long hem?
Is it okay for me to go there?	Hemi olraet sapos mi go long ples ia?
Is it okay for me to look at it?	Hemi olraet sapos mi lukem samting ia?

The Vanuatu Kaljoral Senta, 'Vanuatu Cultural Centre', in the main street of Port Vila is a popular port of call for many visitors. Extensive displays highlight the depth and richness of traditional Vanuatu.

HEALTH

Vanuatu has its main hospital in Port Vila. There are a number of other regional hospitals and medical centres. Not all islands or regions may have a hospital, but most have at least a dispensary, with a nurse in attendance.

Where's a/the ...?	... i stap we?
dentist	dokta blong tut
pharmacy	famasi
Can you take me to a doctor/hospital?	Yu save tekem me i go long dokta/hospital?
I need to see a (nurse).	Mi mi mas go lukim wan (nas).
Is there a ... here?	I gat ... i stap long ples ya?
doctor	dokta
hospital	hospital
I'm feeling sick.	Mi harem i no gud.

Do you have any (malaria) medecine?	Yu gat meresin blong (feva)?
My (head) hurts.	(Hed) blong mi i soa.
It hurts here. (indicate)	Hemi soa long ples ya.
I have a tooth ache.	Tut blong mi i soa.

I'm ...   Mi ...
   diabetic   diabetik
   epileptic   epileptik
   asthmatic   asmatik, mi gat sot win
                                (lit: I'm asthmatic, I have
                                short wind/breath)

Useful Words

Western medicine	meresin
dispensary/clinic	dispenseri/klinik
chemist/pharmacy	dragstoa/famasi
traditional medicine	kastom meresin
inject	stikim
dentist	dokta blong tut
injection	stik meresin
malaria	feva
dengue fever	denggi

BISLAMA

OFF LIMITS

One term that will often be heard around Vanuatu is tambu (or tabu) 'off limits'. The phrase Hemi tambu blong go insaed means 'entry is forbidden'.

When used in relation to custom, tambu may refer to things like places, objects, activities, words, and so on. While it's relatively uncommon for visitors to encounter kastom tambu, particularly around Port Vila, always be sensitive to the situation. If there's any cause for doubt, simply ask.

TIME & DATES

Days and months are the same as in English, but spoken with the influence of local sound patterns.

Days

Monday	Mande
Tuesday	Tusde
Wednesday	Wenesde
Thursday	Tosde
Friday	Fraede
Saturday	Sarede
Sunday	Sande

Months

January	Jenuware
February	Februari
March	Maj
April	Epril
May	Mei
June	Jun
July	Julae
August	Ogis
September	Septemba
October	Oktoba
November	Novemba
December	Desemba

Telling the Time

What's the time?	Wanem taem ya?
It's six o'clock.	Hemi stret long (siks o klok).
It's ...	Hemi ...
twenty minutes past five	twenty minit i lusem faev
nine thirty	teti minti i lusem naen
It's ten to three.	Hemi ten minit i go ronem tri.

Don't be surprised if you regularly hear the time told in English fashion.

NUMBERS

Numbers are as in English, but spoken with the influence of local sound patterns.

1	wan	16	sikstin
2	tu	17	seventin
3	tri	18	eitin
4	fo	19	naentin
5	faev	20	twante
6	siks	30	teti
7	seven	40	foti
8	eit	50	fifti
9	naen	60	siksti
10	ten	70	seventi
11	leven	80	eiti
12	twelef	90	naenti
13	tetin	100	(wan)handred
14	fotin	1000	taosan
15	fiftin	1,000,000	milian

BISLAMA

EMERGENCIES

I'll call the police.	Mbae mi singaot long polis.
I/we want to go to the (police).	Mi/mifala i wantem go long polis.
I/we need a (doctor).	Mi/mifala i nidim dokta.
I/we have to got to the (hospital).	Mi/mifala i mas go long (hospital).
Is there a telephone here?	I gat telefon i stap?
Sorry, but I'm not interested in it.	Sore, be mi gat intres long hem.
Leave me alone.	Livem mi.
I don't want to.	Mi no wantem.
Don't talk to me.	Yu no tok tok long mi.
Could you please help me?	Yu save givhan long mi?
Do you speak English?	Yu save tok tok long Inglis?

FURTHER READING

Camden, W., (1977). *A descriptive dictionary: Bislama to English*. Port Vila: Maropa Bookshop.

Crowley, T., (1990). *Beach-la-mar to Bislama: The emergence of a national language in Vanuatu*. Oxford: Clarendon Press.

Crowley, T., (1994). Practical issues in Bislama Lexicography. *Language and Linguistics in Melanesia*, 25, 1, 27-53.

Crowley, T., (1995). *A New Bislama Dictionary*. Languages Unit, University of the South Pacific. Maryborough, Vic.: Australian Print Group.

Tryon, D., (1986). Neologisms in Bislama (Vanuatu). In J. A. Fishman (Ed.), *The Fergusonian impact: in honor of Charles A Ferguson* Vol 2 (pp 305-313). Berlin: Moulton de Gruyter.

BISLAMA

Solomon Islands Pijin

SOLOMON ISLANDS PIJIN

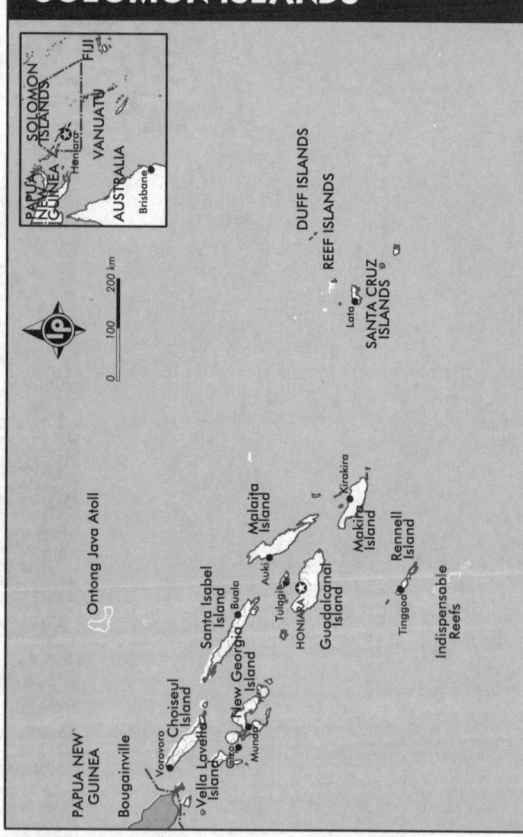

SOLOMON ISLANDS

SOLOMON ISLANDS PIJIN

INTRODUCTION

Solomon Islands Pijin, usually just called Pijin, is a blend of mostly English words modified to fit Melanesian sounds, together with a mix of English and Melanesian grammar. The primary means of communication among people from different language areas, it is the first language of more than 5% of the population. Despite English being taught in all schools, Pijin is the spoken language of the playground, dormitories, businesses, and even government offices. Although still not considered suitable by many for written purposes, the New Testament of the Bible is available in Pijin and the Old Testament is in preparation.

While some Pijin was present in the Solomons as early as the 1860s, it emerged as a lingua franca when labourers started returning from the cane fields of Australia near the end of that century. It has grown steadily both in complexity and usage ever since.

Although some 95% of the vocabulary comes from English, many words have very different meanings. Olketa and oloketa from English 'altogether', have four different meanings between them, none of them being 'altogether'. Olketa/oloketa makes a following noun plural, means 'they/them' as a pronoun, and means 'you' as a term of address. As an exclamation, !Oloketa! means 'wow'.

Influence of local languages causes Pijin to vary alot from area to area. Honiara Pijin and radio Pijin have considerably more English influence than that of rural areas. The radio, however, is helping to standardise usage and a survey done in the 1980s indicates that Honiara Pijin is widely considered the standard.

Listening to the service messages to rural areas on the radio each evening is a good way to learn some Pijin and local culture, since each message is read as it was written in English and then translated into Pijin. Try tuning in.

Pijin is a neat language and although you can get by in most places without it, most people tend to be more relaxed and open if you use it. The basics can be learned in a short time.

SOLOMON ISLANDS PIJIN

A side benefit of knowing a little Pijin, if you're white, is that you'll know when you're the topic of a conversation, or the butt of a joke, if you hear waetman or araikwao, both meaning 'whiteman'.

PRONUNCIATION

Pijin pronunciation is not really difficult for the English speaker since most of the Pijin sounds also occur in English. The most important thing to remember is that in most words, the vowel sounds are pronounced differently to their English equivalents. Pijin pronunciation varies a lot because most speakers bend sounds a little to fit those of their own native languages. For the same reason, they won't be surprised if you bend Pijin a little to fit English sounds.

Vowels

Pijin has five vowels, pronounced much like the sounds of the same letters in German, Spanish, and Italian.

a   as the 'a' in 'father'
e   as the 'e' in 'bet'
i   as the 'ee' in 'beet'
o   as the 'o' in 'gone'
u   as the 'oo' in 'goon'

When two different vowels are joined, both vowels are pronounced. Doubled vowels have a longer vowel sound than single ones. When the letter i begins a word and is followed by another vowel it's pronounced as 'y', as in ies meaning, 'yes'.

IMPORTANT

Always pronounce each vowel according to the pronunciation guide and not how the same letter sounds in English.

Consonants

Most consonants and consonant clusters are acceptable pronounced as in English. A few need special attention.

k, p, t	like English, but without the puff of air that follows them in English
b, mb	like English, but you may hear them both as b or both as mb (as the 'mb' in 'number')
d, nd	like English, but you may hear them both as d or both as nd
g, ngg	g as in 'go', never like 'j' and ngg as 'ng' in 'finger', but you may hear both as g or both as ngg
ng	as 'ng' in 'singer'
r	a single flap of the tongue or trilled like a Spanish 'r'
j	as in English, but you may also hear it pronounced as 's'

Don't be surprised when you hear speakers add a weak vowel between the consonants of a cluster or at the end of words. For example blong can be bilong/bolong or blongo. This is because most of the local languages don't have consonant clusters or word-final consonants.

Stress in Pijin is similar English but it's very important that a 'yes/no' question has a clear rising intonation, since this is often the only clue that it's a question.

DID YOU KNOW ... Kilim dae can signify various means of killing, not uniquely hitting.

GRAMMAR

Many people think that Pijin doesn't have a grammar. Think again. However it's not difficult to learn. The grammar is as rigorous as English, simpler in many areas but more complex in others, such as pronouns. What's important is to keep your ears open and your mouth ready to communicate, even if you make mistakes.

SOLOMON ISLANDS PIJIN

SOLOMON ISLANDS PIJIN

Word Order
Basic sentence structure is the same as English: subject + verb + object.

Daddy will kill the shark.   Dadi bae kilim dae sak ia.
(lit: daddy he hit dead shark the)

Nouns
Nouns aren't marked for number. The indefinite wanfala or the plural olketa may precede a noun in order to clarify this. Speakers sometimes use s for plural as in English or may even use both olketa and s, but if a word like staka meaning 'many' precedes a noun, olketa is not used.

boy	boe; wanfala boe
boys	boe; olketa boe; boes; olketa boes
many boys	staka boe/boes

Articles
Nouns are frequently followed by ia. It is pronounced like part of the preceding word and can be translated as 'the', 'this' or 'that' in English.

Daddy killed the shark.   Dadi hemi kilim dae sak ia.

Adjectives
You're lucky! The biggest difference between Pijin and English is that short adjectives usually have the suffix -fala which simply means hey, I'm an adjective. In this sense cardinal numbers can also be treated as adjectives.

small mango	smolfala manggo
two mangoes	tufala manggo
My mango is big.	Manggo blong mi hemi bikfala.

Important intensifiers are barava meaning 'really' preceding an adjective, and tumas or fogud both meaning 'very', put at the end of a phrase.

really good boy	barava gudfala boe
That boy is really good.	Boe ia hemi barava gudfala.

| very good boy | bikfala boe tumas/fogud |
| That boy is very small. | Boe ia hemi smolfala tumas/fogud. |

Comparisons can be made by using winim meaning 'win'. Winim isn't normally used if the meaning is already clear.

This is the bigger one/biggest one.	Diswan nao hemi bikwan.
Your knife is sharper than mine.	Naef blong iu hemi sap winim naef blong mi.
	(lit: knife of you it sharp winning knife of me)

Pronouns

Singular		
1st person	I	mi
2nd person	you	iu
3rd person	he/she/it	hem
Plural		
1st person exclusive		
we (two)		mitufala
we (three)		mitrifala
we (more than three)		mifala
1st person inclusive		
we (two)		iumitufala
I and you (three)		iumitrifala
I and you (more than three)		iumi
2nd person		
you (two)		iutufala
you (three)		iutrifala
you (more than three)		iufala
3rd person		
they (two)		tufala
they (three)		trifala
they (more than three)		olketa

SOLOMON ISLANDS PIJIN

The Pijin pronoun system is more complex than that of English. In addition to singular and plural, Pijin has pronouns referring to two and even three persons or things. The trickiest part is that you have to not only specify whether it is one, two, three or more, but also whether the person you're speaking to is included (inclusive) or not (exclusive).

When used as the subject all except mi, iu and iumi may also be followed by i (pronounced 'ee') which can't be translated into English. The i basically marks the end of the subject and the beginning of the predicate in a sentence. Except for hemi, the i is written as a separate word. When a noun is the subject, a pronoun normally follows the noun.

John went to Honiara.	Jon hemi goap long Honiara.
Henry and Alice went to Tambea.	Henri an Alis tufala i godaon long Tambea.
	(lit: Henry and Alice they-two i went-down to Tambea)

Possessive pronouns are easy – just put blong before the possesor and that's it.

my basket	basket blong mi
our (exclusive pl) father	dadi blong mifala

Verbs

Verbs aren't difficult – no conjugations, but there are some tricky particles.

Tense

There are only two tenses, future and non-future. Future tense is signaled by bae or baebae which comes early in the sentence. Non-future is not marked in any way although some specific time word may be included (see page 91).

I'll go to Auki.	Bae/baebae mi go long Auki.
I went to Auki/I'm going to Auki.	Mi go long Auki.
I went to Auki last week.	Mi go long Auki las wik.

Transitive & Intransitive

Pijin has both transitive and intransitive verbs, but unlike English, transitive verbs can't be changed to passive verbs, as Pijin has no passive voice.

Intransitive verbs have no object, and many nouns such as holide 'holiday', can be used as intransitive verbs.

I will go to Isabel.	Bae mi go long Isabel
I will take my vacation on Isabel.	Bae mi holide long Isabel.
I'm going to have a shower/bath.	Bae mi suim nao.

Transitive verbs have either an expressed or implied object and are marked with a suffix which can be -em, -im, -um, or -m. The suffix rules are complex, but don't worry, if you get them wrong you'll be understood. A few transitive verbs like save (related to English savvy), meaning 'know', don't have a suffix.

Mum is bathing the baby.	Mami hemi suimim bebi.
They sell bicycles in Chinatown.	Olketa salem baesikol long Saenataon.
I don't know anything.	Mi no save enisamting.

NO KAN DO

A common mistake made by English speakers is to use kan for 'can'. It means 'can't'.

Preverb Particles

Preverb particles are particles that precede verbs.

must	mas
should	sud
want to	laek/laekem/wande/wandem
can	save

can't	kanduit; no save; kan; kanot
about to	kolsap
just (indicating time)	jes

| I can't go today. | Mi kanduit go tude. |
| The service is about to start. | Prea hemi kolsap stat nao. |

Postverb Particles

Postverb particles follow verbs. Two postverb directionals are kam and go signalling direction toward or away from the speaker, respectively. They are extremely common with verbs involving motion, transfer or exchange but have no English counterpart.

| Tell me. | Talem kam long mi. |
| Tell Mary. | Talem go long Meri. |

Two other postverb particles not usually translated into English are:

- Nao which makes the verb the focal point of the sentence and can often signal completion. Any part of the sentence can be marked with nao.

Daddy will kill the shark.	Dadi nao bae kilim dae sak ia.
Daddy will kill the *shark*.	Dadi bae kilim dae sak ia nao.
Let's go!	!Iumi muv nao!

- ia which gives a slight emphasis (also see page 58).

| He went! | !Hemi go ia! |

A really tricky, but very common, postverb particle is nomoa meaning 'just/only'. It comes from English 'no more', but means almost the opposite. The biblical admonition of Jesus to a woman he forgave to go and sin no more sounds to the Pijin speaker like !Go an sin nomoa! meaning 'go and do nothing but sin'.

SOLOMON ISLANDS PIJIN

To Be

Pijin has no verb 'to be'. Often nothing is used, but to indicate location, a preposition, or the verb stap, meaning 'to stay' may be used. This indicates existence.

I'm a student.	Mi wanfala stiuden.
They're very happy.	Olketa hapi tumas.
Manu is in Honiara.	Manu hemi long Honiara.
Is the priest in?	?Mama stap?
There are still some sweet potatoes.	Kumara stap iet.

Negatives

There are several negative words. Some are listed above as preverb particles since they are combined with a particle to mean can't (see page 61).

No.	No/Nomoa.
Certainly not!	!Nating/Nating nao/Nomoa nao!
That man does not like to travel by ship.	Man ia, hemi no laek fo go long sip.
That man does not like to travel by ship!	!Man ia, hemi nating laek fo go long sip!

Questions

Questions are written in Pijin with a question mark at the beginning and end of a sentence, so the reader will know what intonation to use before he starts the question. This is crucial for the many yes/no questions signalled only by intonation.

who	hu
what	wanem
when	wataem
why	waswe
where	wea
which	watkaen
how	hao
how much	haomas
how many	haomeni

A question word beginning a sentence is normally followed by nao, marking it as the topic. Some question words may also be used at the end of a sentence.

Where are you going?	?Wea nao iu go/Iu go wea?
Who took my basket?	?Hu nao tekem basket blong mi?
What is it like?	?Hemi olsem wanem?

Yes/No Questions

Although signalled by a rising intonation, to avoid being misunderstood it's safer to also start the question with waswe which literally means 'why'. They also may be followed by nomoa meaning 'just/only' or o nomoa meaning 'or not'.

Are you going to the market?	?Bae iu go long maket; Waswe, bae you go long maket?
Do you live nearby?	?Iu stap kolsap; Iu stap kolsap o nomoa?
Are you all right?	?Iu oraet nomoa; Waswe, iu oraet nomoa?

A special yes/no question asking for confirmation ends with ia man meaning 'isn't that so' (lit: yes man). It doesn't matter whether the addressee is man, woman or child.

Solomon Islands is a great country, isn't it?	?Solomon Aelan hemi barava gudfala kandre, ia man?

Yes.	Ies/Ia.
No.	Nomoa.
Not yet.	No moa iet.
Perhaps.	Ating.
I don't know.	Mi no save tu.

The use of no ... tu meaning 'not ... either' in the last example assumes the questioner doesn't know the answer either.

Prepositions

The three true prepositions must have an expressed object. These are the general prepositions long with a wide range of meaning, blong meaning 'of', and fo meaning 'for/to'.

The girl went to Honiara.	Gele ia hemi go long Honiara.
I'm staying at the hotel.	Mi stap long hotel.
Give the mango to Helen.	Givim go manggo ia fo/long Helen.
Naha is a part of Honiara.	Naha hemi wanfala eria blong Honiara.

Verbal prepositions are like mermaids, half verb and half preposition. They end with the transitive suffix m and, like a transitive verb, don't have to have an expressed object if one is already implied (see page 61).

May I go with you (sg)?	?Waswe, mi save go wetem iu?
You (pl) get out of here/there!	!Iufala goaot from!

Some verbal prepositions are:

with	wetem	about	abaotem
against	agensim	from	from

Conjunctions

and	an
but	bat
or	o
if	sapos
therefore	olsem
because/since	bikos
that	wea/dat
then (temporal)	bihaen/(long)taem ia/den
before	bifoa
so/in order that	so/mekem

| I know that it isn't far away. | Mi save wea/dat hemi no farawe. |
| Wake up quickly so you (sg) and I can go. | Wekap kuiktaem mekem iumitufala save go. |

MEETING PEOPLE

Solomon Islanders are friendly and usually easy to meet. Diverse in culture and speaking many different languages, Pijin binds them all. Most are shy to initiate a conversation with outsiders because of the language barrier. So although many do understand English, learning some Pijin and initiating a conversation really makes a difference.

IT'S IN THE EYES

Remember, eye contact is unusual for Solomon Islanders so don't be put off if people don't look at you when your talking to them. Personal space is also important so don't stand or sit too close.

SOLOMON ISLANDS PIJIN

Greetings & Civilities

People nod their heads, wave and smile when they meet friends or relatives, or just say ?Hao?, meaning 'how's it going'. If you've been away for a while and meet friends and relatives, a handshake is normal. Those who are obviously elderly can be respectfully addressed as olo, literally meaning old. A mature woman can be politely addressed as mami meaning 'mother', a man as dadi meaning 'father'. Males can address other males they know as bro meaning 'brother'. If in doubt, fren or maefren meaning 'friend' is acceptable.

Good morning.	Moning/Mone.
	(you may hear gud moning, but this may be someone's best English used for your benefit)
Good morning.	Mone, mone, mone; Moning; Mone.
	(in response)
Good afternoon.	Aftanun.
Good evening.	Ivining.
	(when you can still see the person)
Good evening.	Gudnaet.
	(after dark and used whether the person can be seen or not)
Hello friend.	Halo fren/maefren.
How are you?	?Hao/Oraet nomoa?
Fine.	Oraet nomoa.
So, so.	Olsem nomoa.

SOLOMON ISLANDS PIJIN

SMELLY BRUCE

Beware! If your name is Bruce, be prepared with an alternative or for sniggering. Brus, pronounced 'Bruce', means fart.

Special terms, identical with the third person pronouns, are used for greeting two, three, or a number of people.

Good morning to you (two/three/more than three).
Mone/Moning/tufala/trifala/olketa.

BODY LANGUAGE

Although Solomon Islanders avoid eye contact, one neat custom is greeting people by raising the eyebrows and making fleeting eye contact. It can be used whether you know the person or not and is especially handy when talking while walking with a person want to acknowledge someone approaching you.

From further away, you can greet people with a wave of the hand or a nod of the head. If walking in the dark when you meet people, !Gudnaet! meaning 'good evening', is the appropriate, and reassuring, greeting. Small children love to be greeted with a simple !Babae! meaning 'bye-bye' and waving to them.

Goodbyes

I have to go.	Bae mi go nao.
See you (sg) later!	!Lukim iu (bihaen)!
See you (pl) tomorrow!	!Lukim iufala tumoro!

First Encounters

If you want to get acquainted with someone, say !Halo!, and introduce yourself to start a conversation. It's proper to give your name and ask the other person his/her name.

My name is (Robert).	Nem blong mi (Robet).
Say it again.	Talem kam moa.
I can't hear you clearly.	Mi no herem iu gud.
What's your name?	?Hu nao nem blong iu?
Pleased to meet you.	Mi hapi tumas fo mitim iu.

How old are you?	?Iu kasem haomas iia?
I'm 40.	Mi kasem foti nomoa.
Are you married (yet)?	?Waswe, iu marit iet?
No, I'm not married yet.	Nomoa, mi no marit iet.
Yes, I'm married.	Ia, mi marit finis.
Where is your wife/ husband from?	?Iu marit long wea?
I am married to a (New Zealander).	Mi marit long (Niu Silan).

Cultural expectations are that everyone will marry so it's appropriate
to use iet in both the question and answer above.

Nationalities

You'll find that many country names in Pijin are very similar to
English. If your country is not listed below try saying it in English
and you'll most likely be understood.

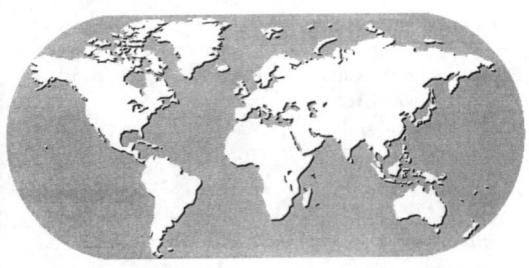

Where are you from?	?Iu kam from wea?
I'm from...	Mi kam from...
America	Merika/Amerika
Australia	Ostrelia
England	Ingglan
Germany	Jemani
New Zealand	Niu Silan

Family

mother	mami
father	dadi
child	pikinini
daughter	gele
son	boe
sister	sista
brother	brata
wife	waef/misis blong (mi)
husband	hasban/olo blong (mi)

Useful Phrases

How many children do you have?	?Hao mas pikinini nao iu garem?
I don't have any children yet.	Mi no garem eni pikinini iet.
I have (three) children, (one boy) and (two girls).	Mi garem (trifala) pikinini nomoa, (wanfala boe) an (tufala gele).
How many brothers and sisters do you have?	?Hao mas brata an sista nao iu garem?
(One) sister and (two) brothers.	(Wanfala) sista an (tufala) brata.
I am the ...	mi nao ...
oldest	fasbon
second born	sekonbon
youngest	lasbon
Are your parents still living?	?Waswe, mami an dadi blong iu laef iet?
(My mother) is still living.	(Mami) blong iu hemi laef iet.
(My father) has been dead a long time.	(Dadi) blong mi hemi dae longtaem kam nao.
Both of them are still living.	Tufala evriwan i laef iet.

Extended Family

Solomon Islanders are extended family oriented, but how they are related can be very confusing. Let's prepare to meet some of these relatives.

aunt	mami/anti
nephew	pikinini/boe/ (smol) anggol/anti
niece	pikinini/gele/ (smol) anggol/anti
cousin (father's brother's son/mother's sister's son)	brata
cousin (mother's sister's daughter/ father's brother's daughter)	sista
cousin (father's sister's children and mother's brother's children)	kasin/kasin sista/kasin brata
grandparent	(olo) grani
grandchild	(smol) grani
grandfather	grandadi
grandmother	granmami
in-law	inlo/tambu
father in-law	dadi inlo
mother in-law	mami inlo

You may also hear the less common san and dota for 'son' and 'daughter' and nefiu and nis for 'nephew' and 'niece'.

Some of the kinship terms are reciprocal, that is, the same term is used for two people. Grani means 'grandparent/grandchild', anggol means 'uncle/niece/nephew', and anti means 'aunt/niece'/ 'nephew'. Whether anggol and anti mean 'niece' or 'nephew' depends on the the older person's gender.

For the aunt/uncle and niece/nephew relationships, the terms anti and anggol are somewhat restricted and vary from area to area. In some matrilineal groups, anggol is mother's brother and reciprocally his sister's children and anti, is not used at all. Parent-child terms are used for the others. If you're confused, ask people how they are related.

Do both of you have the same parents?	Waswe, iutufala bon kam long sem dadi an mami o nomoa?
No, he/she was born of my (father's brother).	Nomoa. Hemi bon kam long (brata blong dadi blong mi).
Is (she) your real (mother)?	?Waswe, hemi barava (mami) blong iu?
How many grandchildren do you have?	?Hao mas grani nao iu garem?
I have a lot of grandchildren, perhaps (ten).	Mi staka grani tumas, (tenfala) nao ating.

Meeting Families

First, be sure the head of the family is notified of your coming. If you know about the family through a person not present, you can introduce yourself without having met any members before. Be sure to sit where and how it is appropriate. Don't sit with people of the opposite sex. Modest clothing is expected. It's better to err on the side of being too modest. For women, a skirt and blouse, or dress, not too short, is still best in most villages. You'll notice that when women are sitting they keep the bottom of their skirt pulled tight and tucked in between their legs. For men, shirt (T-shirts OK) and pants, but not too short. Hair should be neat, or they may think you're a rascal. Always show respect to everyone in the family. Ask questions politely. You may be asked a lot of questions about your status in your family, so don't be put off by these.

Sharing small items, especially food, is always appreciated and accepting what is offered is expected.

Ask permission to take photos of family members and if you can, send them copies later. Older people may use the term laekness meaning 'likeness' to refer to a photo.

May I take a photo of your family?	?Waswe, mi save tekem foto/ laekness blong famili blong iu?

FORMAL INTRODUCTIONS

Non-Traditional

In semiformal or formal situations, such as government offices or churches, the meeting is always initiated with a handshake. When meeting government officials, use English. Some take the use of Pijin as patronising. Use the same courtesies in talking with officials as you normally would in a formal situation. In a situation where people are seated, the seating may be by rank, so wait for someone to show you where to sit.

In most situations, men and boys sit together and women and girls sit together. In all churches and most other meeting places besides a few in Honiara, men and women sit on opposite sides of a room, with men being given priority in seating.

If you go to church, people will shake your hand, but unless they know English they may well not say anything more than !God bles iu! meaning 'God bless you' or iumitufala sekhan fastaem meaning 'let's shake hands'. When shaking hands, they may also grasp their (or your) right wrist with their left hand. Don't hesitate to initiate a conversation.

SOLOMON ISLANDS PIJIN

Storytelling

Stories can be told any time people are sitting around relaxing. If you don't hear them, don't hesitate to ask if someone can tell some stories. Listening to stories can be an excellent way to learn Pijin. A good way to hear some is by listenening to the half-hour custom story program on Saturday evening which SIBC (Solomon Islands Broadcasting Corporation) has been airing for more then two decades.

Almost everyone knows some exciting shark stories both from personal experience and from olketa kastom stori meaning 'legends'. Some exciting stories include:

WWII stories	Olketa stori abaotem Bikfala Faet
The giant and two boys	Jaean wetem tufala boe
The dog and the iguana	Dog wetem iguana
How we got the coconut	Hao iumi garem kokonat
The hermit crab and the heron	Kokosu wetem tuu

And if you're brave, people like to hear your legends too.

NO MORE WORDS

Yes/no questions may be answered without words. Raising the eyebrows and/or a slight upward nod is enough for a yes, and a slight shake of the head is enough for a no.

Some rhetorical devices are:

now	nao
all right	oraet
okay	okei
once upon a time	wanfala taem/longtaem go finis
bye and bye; and so it went on	go-go-go
(may be repeated more times)	
until	go-go
then	taem ia; long taem ia; den

Other words you'll hear include:

beach/sand	sanbis
bow and arrow	bou an aro
hermit crab	kokosu
heron	tuu
high tide	hae taed

IN THE VILLAGE

Formal meetings in villages differ from one another because of cultural differences, but generally the chief (or other 'big man' if no chief) must be formally met and notified of your visit and its purpose. If someone has invited you to the village, they should initiate the meeting. Wait for the chief to offer a handshake. Men shouldn't shake hands with a woman unless the chief has given the woman permission. In some areas, a man could be required to pay compensation for tickling a woman's hand. You can acknowledge meeting them with a nod of the head. Women must take care never to walk over the legs of men sitting down.

If you should be lucky enough to meet one of the small Polynesian groups, you may be greeted with a nose kiss (touching noses).

For a formal village meeting, there's normally an exchange of gifts, so you should try to learn ahead of time what would be appropriate. In many villages, betel nut is appropriate, but not in those of some Christian denominations. Gifts of food, especially items like coffee, Milo, sugar, sweet biscuits, tins of dry milk, tins of meat and rice are often appropriate as are small items such as lighters or souvenirs from your home.

I just came from (Australia).	Mi jes kam from (Ostrelia).
We have come to see (Father John) in your village.	Mifala kam fo lukim (Mama Jon) long vilij blong iu.
We have brought a little something for you.	Mifala tekem kam lelebet samting fo iu.
Thank you.	Tanggio tumas.
Thanks for all you've done for us.	Tanggio tumas fo evrisamting iu duim fo mifala.
You're welcome.	No wariwari/wari(s).

SOLOMON ISLANDS PIJIN

low tide	drae wata
machete/bush knife	busnaef
ocean	solwata
shore	soa
to be cross	kros
to go ashore	go soa
to paddle	padol go/waswas
to quarrel/argue	raoa
to shoot	sutim
turtle	totel

Letter Writing

Relax, all business letters are written in English!

Personal letters can be written in Pijin. How to address the person depends on the relationship. Use the same phrases you would use in addressing the person orally. If in doubt, use the person's first name, or fren.

Dia bro ...	Dear brother ... (from a male to a good male friend)
Gudfala mone go long iu.	Good morning to you.
?Iu stap oraet nomoa?	How are you?
Mi stap gud nomoa long hia.	I'm fine here.
Mi hapi tumas fo raetem disfala leta long iu.	I'm very happy to write to you.
Ating hem nomoa mi garem fo talem distaem.	That's all I have to say.
Bae-bae.	Goodbye.
from fren blong iu	from your friend

> **DID YOU KNOW ...** Within a family, in-laws are considered tambu and must be spoken or referred to indirectly. Tambu literally means 'forbidden'.

SOLOMON ISLANDS PIJIN

OUT OF BOUNDS

Some places in a village are out of bounds to anyone except a certain few. This would be true of a place where sacrifices are made in a non-Christian village. Also near most villages there are specific areas of the beach or elsewhere set apart for men and for women, so be careful to find out where you can and can't go.

| Where is the men's/ women's area? | ?Wea nao eria blong olketa man/woman? |

If there's a person of the opposite sex alone in a house, don't go inside. Even certain relatives can't enter in this stuation.

GETTING AROUND

The ways to get from here to there vary from walking to flying, from canoe to boat, and from buses and taxis to trucks.

Finding Your Way

Solomon Islanders will be happy to give you directions, but they can often be quite vague. If directions aren't too clear, go as far as you can and ask again.

NAMBA NAEN

(lit: number nine) was the 9th field hospital during WWII.

Where is a/the ...?	?Wea nao ...?
Central Market	Sentrol Maket
hospital	hospitol/Namba Naen
pharmacy	famasi
post office	pos ofis
supermarket	supamaket
Yacht Club	Iat Klab

SOLOMON ISLANDS PIJIN

Is it nearby/far away?	?Waswe, hemi kolsap/farawe?
It's nearby/far away.	Hemi kolsap/farawe lelebet.
I don't have transportation.	Mi no eni transpot.
How long would it take to walk?	?Hao long nao bae hemi tekem fo wakabaot go?

In town, buildings and trees are common reference points.

It's on the other side of the ...	Hemi long saet go long ...
mango tree	manggo ia
ANZ bank	ANZ bang
It's on this side of (the) ...	Hemi long saet kam ...
rain tree	ren tri ia
Solomon Airlines	Solomon Ealaen
It's near the ...	Hemi kolsap long ...
post office	pos ofis
coconut tree over there	kokonat longwe
It's on the opposite/right/ left side.	Hemi long narasaet/ raetsaet/lefsaet.

EXCLAMATIONS!

Excuse me.	Eskius plis.
My word!	!Maewat!
Crikey!	!Maekrangge!
Really?	?Turu?
Really!	!Turu!
Wow!	!Oloketa!
You're lying!	!Laea!

Taxi

Taxis are generally not expensive. They're regularly inspected for safety, but not for comfort or oomph. Taxis don't have meters and it's wise to ask about fares in advance so that if it's too high, you can bargain a little. Drivers, of course, need to know approximately where you're going before they can give a price. They may ask you to make an offer first hoping you might offer more than they'd ask. Unless you know how much it should be, insist that he make the first offer. They may be offended if you offer too little.

Normally the only way to get a taxi is to flag one down. The Honiara airport and sometimes Central Market are exceptions. Taxis can be hired for longer trips and some drivers make good guides.

What's it cost to go to (the) ...	?Hao mas nao fo go long ...
Kukum police station	Kukim pulis stesin
post office	pos ofis
Panatina Plaza	Panatina Plasa
	(shopping complex)
wharf	waf

It's up to you.	Saet blong iu.
No, you're the one who knows.	Nomoa, iu nao iu save.
Turn left/right here.	Tane lef/raet long hia.
I'll get out at that house.	Bae mi godaon long haos ia.

Buying Tickets

Where can I buy a (boat) ticket for (Gizo)?	?Wea nao mi save peim tiket fo tekem(sip) go long (Giso)?
On what days does the boat go to (Gizo)?	?Watkaen dei nao (sip) hemi go long (Giso)?
What's the fare for ...?	?Hao mas nao fea fo ...?
economy class	ikonomi klas
first class	fas klas
a cabin	kabin
When does the (Iumi Nao) leave?	?Wataem nao (Iumi Nao) hemi aot?

Hire Car

Available at the airport. You don't need Pijin to rent one – money is adequate. A taxi may be cheaper even for sightseeing and as mentioned, taxi drivers can make good guides. Be prepared for congestion in and out of the downtown area. There are no traffic lights and no stop signs. Yield when coming onto a main road from a feeder road.

Bus

Buses, mostly a species of minibus, are numerous in Honiara, cheap to ride, and a good place to meet people and practice Pijin. Fares in urban areas bus are one price, regardless of destination. There are very few out of town buses.

Where's the bus stop?	?Wea nao bas stop?
It's over there.	Hemi longwe.
How much is the fare?	Hao mas nao bas fea?
Which bus do I take to go to (Chinatown)?	?Watkaen bas nao bae mi tekem fo kasem (Saenataon)?
Any bus is all right.	Eni bas nomoa hemi oraet.
You need to take the (KG VI) bus.	Iu mas tekem (KG Sikis) bas.

Schedules are indefinite, but there are usually a couple of trips in the morning and a couple in the afternoon. Inbound buses leave early in the morning and afternoon and outbound buses later. These buses are mainly used by people living along the bus routes.

Truck

Where there are roads but no buses, inquire about the possibility of getting on a truck.

Where can I find a truck to (Lambi Bay)?	?Wea nao mi save faendem trak fo go long (Lambi Bei)?

Canoe

Some places are accessible only by canoe. You can arrange for a canoe with outboard and a driver (draeva) to go to various places. A good example is getting to Savo from Honiara to see the hot springs and megapod fields (organised tours are also available). If you aren't used to riding in a canoe, you may be in for a thrill and possibly a spill if the landing is rough. Provide your own life jacket and make sure your camera or video are in watertight containers that float. Enquire at the Yacht Club or Central Market for canoes bound for Savo and other places. Considering the distance, canoe travel is relatively expensive.

I want to go to (Savo) tomorrow.	Mi laek go long (Savo) tumoro.
Where can I find a canoe and driver?	?Wea nao mi save faendem kanu wetem draeva?
What will it cost me?	?Hao mas nao bae hemi kostem mi?
What do I need to take with me?	?Watkaen samting nao mi mas tekem go?
How long will it take to get to (Savo)?	?Hao long nao bae hemi tekem fo kasem (Savo)?
How long will we be able to stay in (Savo)?	?Hao long nao bae iumi save stap long (Savo)?

SOLOMON ISLANDS PIJIN

Boat

Boat travel is the main means of transport and can be a lot of fun. There are some passenger boats and a good number of cargo boats which take passengers. Each company has its own office and destinations. Many of the trips will be at night, especially departures from Honiara going to ports that take most of the night, or longer, to reach. An exception is Ocean Express, a passenger boat which travels only in daylight. The Ocean Express is fast, but confining like an airplane – no deck and little space for luggage.

Boat fares aren't expensive. Normally tickets need to be purchased in advance, except when space is available at small ports en route. Some boats have soft drinks and snacks available, but basically passengers are responsible for food, and for sleeping mats to spread out on deck. Some boats have cabins, but these may be hot if not air-conditioned.

Strictly passenger boats try to adhere to schedules, although weather and other factors can make changes. Schedules for other boats are very flexible – more likely delayed than early (not always), and frequently cancelled. Don't take a boat to a place that's not easy to get to and expect to return on schedule. You could get stuck somewhere for a long time, like months!

You don't really need Pijin for the shipping offices, but try it anyway. The deck is the real place to practise Pijin.

When will we arrive at (Auki)?	?Wataem nao bae iumi kasem (Auki)?
What island is that?	?Watkaen aelan nao?
What's that over there?	?Wanem nao long dea?
They're dolphins.	Olketa dolfin nao ia.
Where's the toilet?	?Wea nao toelet?
I'm seasick.	Mi siksik.
I'm going to throw up.	Bae mi toroaot.
Where are we?	?Iumi kasem long wea?
How long will we be here?	?Hao long nao bae iumi stap long hia?
Is it OK to go ashore?	?Waswe, hemi oraet fo gosoa?

Air

Save your Pijin. Unless they know you've been around a long time, agents at Solomon Airlines and other travel agencies in Honiara will speak English with you anyway. At small agencies elsewhere, Pijin might be helpful but not normally necessary.

Air travel is considerably more expensive than boat, except for a couple of flights from Honiara to the Weather Coast of Guadalcanal, where the flights are short. Planes tend to adhere to schedules, so don't be late unless you clearly know of a delay.

FOOD

Local fruits and vegetables can be bought at the markets in urban areas. Red meat and dressed chicken can be bought at butcher shops, supermarkets or in Chinese shops. Fish, and sometimes live chickens, shellfish and crabs, can be bought at the market. Fish may be weighed either in kilos or pounds.

You need to provide your own containers at the market, but you can buy various sizes of plastik, 'plastic bags', there. Be sure to go armed with enough coins, and small notes as vendors are often unable to make change.

Be careful what you buy. One traveller bought a parcel of banana leaves thinking it was prepared food wrapped in the leaves!

At the Market

Prices per piece, bundle or heap, are usually written on scraps of cardboard, but if not you can point and ask. Just select what you want and put it in your basket. Unless very young, market women can be addressed as mami

How much (is this; are these)?	?Hao mas nao diswan/datwan?
Can you change a five?	?Waswe, iu save senisim faev dola?
Whose pineapples are these?	?Paenapol blong hu ia?
What's this?	?Wanem nao diswan?
Is this edible?	?Waswe, diswan hemi fo kaikai?
I don't want this/that.	Mi no wandem diswan/datwan.

SOLOMON ISLANDS PIJIN

| I want to (buy) this/that. | Mi laek (baem/peim) diswan/datwan. |
| Hand me the other one so I can look at it. | Kam narawan mekem mi lukim. |

Fruit & Nuts

banana	banana (if large and very firm, they are likely cooking bananas)
betel nut	bilnat
bush apple	busapol (light greenish fruit sometimes with tinges of red)
bush lime	buslaem (good for juice if not too small or too hard)
canarium nut	nalinat (sold already shelled)
cantaloupe	rokmelon
orange	orens (sometimes very sour)
pamelo	pamolo (a big citrus fruit, but usually good)
papaya/pawpaw	popo
peanut	pinat
pineapple	paenapol
star fruit	faev kona

Common Vegetables & Tubers

capsicum/green pepper	kapsikam
cassava/manioc	kai bia; kasava
green beans	bin
green leafy vegetables	kavis
head cabbage	bol kavis
leaf for eating with betel nut	lif
shallot	salat
slippery cabbage	slipri kavis
sweet potato	kumara
taro	taro
yam	iam (dark rough skinned tuber; tastes much like white potatoes)
yam	pana (light brownish tuber)

Seafood & Chicken

chicken	kokorako
crab	krab
fish	fis
reef fish	rif fis
tuna	bonito

FAVOURITE THINGS

Tinned tuna called taio may not sound traditional, but it is a favourite of Solomon Islanders and they would think of it as traditional. Solomon Blue, the dark meat, is especially popular and less expensive than the white meat, which is tinned mostly for export. It's used for protein in many dishes.

In the Shop

Do you have (plain flour)?	?Waswe, iufala garem (plen flaoa)?
Do you sell (matches)?	?Waswe, iufala salem (masis)?

Weights & Measures

Weights may be either in pounds or kilos depending on the type of scales. Most stores and butchers now have only kilo scales, but some fish vendors still sell by the pound.

Lengths may be metric or imperial. Fabric is often sold in precut lengths of one fathom (two yards) for the traditional **lavalava** a wrap-around skirt worn by men and women at home.

Liquid volume is measured by the litre although kerosene is often sold in small soft drink bottles. Most measurements are pronounced in a similar way to English.

bottle of kerosene	botol karasin
pound	paon
two pounds	tu/tufala paon

kilo	kilo
five kilos	faev/faefala kilo
gram	gram
500 grams	faev handred gram

Traditional Cooking

Each island has its own way of cooking food. The ingredients might be the same or slightly different, but cooking methods differ. Names of similar dishes also vary, so don't hesitate to ask about names.

One of the most common but delightfully rich ingredients of Solomon Islands cooking is milk blong kokonat, that is, coconut cream. It's produced by grating husked coconuts which have been broken in half and then, after thoroughly mixing the grated coconut in a little water, squeezing the liquid from the grated coconut. The coconut cream is used to season foods cooked in many different ways. If you get a chance, ask someone to show you how to husk and scrape a coconut.

Many traditional foods are cooked in a stone or earth oven. All kinds of foods are wrapped in banana or other large leaves to be baked in the ovens including pork, chicken, fish, sweet potatoes and other tubers and various kinds of greens called kavis. Thick coconut cream may be added before wrapping. You may not be treated to these traditional foods, however, unless you are invited to a home to eat, to a church dinner or to a feast.

Traditional puddings are also baked in the stone oven. For these any of various tubers can be grated but cassava is the most common. Thick coconut cream is mixed into the grated tuber before enclosing it in the leaves. Nuts, bananas or fish may be added to the pudding.

Pudding is a must for feasts. In some areas, puddings are stored underground to age for several months. You may hear of three or six month pudding from Makira. On the remote islands of Tikopia and Anuta, it's stored for use during cyclones.

The fruit of the mangrove tree is used to make a dish called koa'a. The inside of the long round pod is scraped out with a seashell. After washing and boiling the flesh, coconut cream along with fish or shellfish and vegetables are added. It may also have mashed pumpkin added for flavour and may be baked in a stone oven.

A very tasty way of cooking some foods such as fish, pork, grated taro and canarium nuts is in freshly cut bamboo. The bamboo containing the food is then 'burned' on the fire. Other foods are cooked directly on the fire in a process called bonebone literally 'burn-burn'.

In some areas sharks, crocodiles and certain birds may be forbidden for eating if considered to be the ancestral totem of the people.

Traditional cooking does not include desserts, except cake on occasions such as marriage feasts, but cordial, drinking coconuts, or a hot drink may be served after eating. Many meals will be followed by eating the narcotic betel nuts and storytelling.

How do you cook it?	?Hao nao iu kukim?
stone/earth oven	motu/korongis
bake in a stone oven	motum/korongisim
husk a coconut	haskem kokonat
grate a coconut	skrasim kokonat
coconut cream	milk/melek blong kokonat
to add coconut cream to	milkim/melekem
to cut in pieces	pisisim
to peel	skinim/pilam
to wrap in leaves	paselem/paselem long lif
cassava; taro pudding	kasava; taro puding

Modern Dishes

Mostly western type dishes are served in restaurants and they are listed in English on the menus. In Chinese restaurants they are in both English and Chinese. In snack bars, sometimes called kai baa, the items will normally be displayed and labelled along with prices. Popular items are fish and chips, grilled reef fish, prawns, roast chicken, and imported beef steak. In the kai baa or snack bar, curried dishes with rice and sandwiches are popular, along with a tasty roti made of available local foods such as pumpkin, eggplant and mince rolled up in a flour tortilla.

Most chips are made from sweet potatoes. They're good, just not the same those made from white potatoes.

BETEL NUT

Bia Blong Solomon (Solomons' beer) is what islanders light-heartedly call the nut of the areca palm. The meat of the betel nut is chewed in a betel-pepper leaf with lime. It has a mildly intoxicating and tonic effect caused by the catalytic effect of nut, leaf and lime. Betel nut chewers usually carry a lime box with leaves.

The nut is best chewed when the fruit is green and soft and juicy in the husk. First bite off the top of the nut then hold it sideways between you teeth and bite it open. After this, roll up the leaf and chew it. Finally use a spatula or finger to put the lime in your mouth.

The lime eventually eats away the chewer's gums and can cause serious mouth ulcers, especially among people who chew 10 or more betel nuts a day. Nearly 20% of all local cancer cases – about 30 people per year – are associated with chewing betel nut.

Eating Out

English is generally understood by those who work in the restaurants, but you may like to try some phrases. It's OK to introduce yourself too.

I want to book a table
(for four).
What do you have on
your menu for today?

Mi laek fo bukim wanfala
tebol (fo fofala).
?Wanem nao iufala garem long
lis fo kaikai tude?

What do you have to drink?	?Watkaen dring nao iufala garem?
I want ...	Mi laekem ...
Do you have beer?	?Waswe, iu eni bia?

Traditional dishes are not normally served in restaurants, but may be available on special nights such as a weekly island night. Try asking some of the following questions:

Do you have ...?	?Waswe, iufala garem ...?
an island night	aelan naet
traditional/local/island food	kastom/lokol/aelan kaikai
food cooked in a stone oven	kaikai wea olketa motum
pudding baked in a stone oven	puding wea olketa motum
food cooked with coconut cream	kaikai wea olketa milkim/melekem

FESTIVALS
There are many festivals and holidays in the Solomon Islands, but traditional ones vary a lot from area to area. Festivals and holidays celebrated widely are either religious and/or ones proclaimed by the government.

Holidays
Church holidays include Christmas, Easter, and Pentecost along with festivals for Saints Days (some churches), ordinations, baptisms, confirmations, marriages, and jubilees. If you happen to be in an area when one of these are being celebrated, you'll have an excellent opportunity to observe current celebrations.

Most feasts are accompanied by local dances known as kastom danis. Celebrations are characterised by speeches. In the villages they may be in the language of the area. Otherwise, they will be in a mixture of Pijin and English and you should be able to understand a lot if you listen carefully.

National holidays not of a religious origin are New Years, Independence and the Queen's Birthday. The Solomon Islands observes eight legal national holidays. Easter and Pentecost are not included since they always fall on Sunday. If a legal holiday falls on a weekend, it will be observed on Friday or Monday, with most businesses observing the holidays. Christmas is the biggest holiday nationwide with carolling before and after widespread. Most people take their annual holiday and go to their home islands making Honiara quieter, although it becomes harder to get things processed in government offices. Some businesses close for 10 days or more and some people take a Makira holide, that is, an extended holiday without permission.

New Years	Niu Iia
Good Friday	Gud Fraede
Easter Monday	Ista Mande
Whit Monday	Wit Mande (dei
(day after Pentecost)	bihaen Pentekos)
Queen's Birthday	Betde blong Kuin (mektu
(2nd Friday of June)	Fraede long Jun)
Independence	Independens (7 Julae)
Christmas	Krismas
Thanksgiving/Boxing Day	Dei blong Tanggio/
	Bokising Dei

Officially Boxing Day has been changed to Thanksgiving, but most people still call it Bokising Dei.
Each province has a legal holiday called Appointed Day which is celebrated in the provincial capitals.

(local) dance	(kastom) danis
(western) dance	hula
feast	fist
invited guests	olketa invaeted ges
marriage feast	marit fist
MC	MC
prayer	prea
speech	toktok
speaker	spika
wedding	marit

Hip, hip, hurrah!	!Hip, hip, hure!
Let's end with three happy cheers.	Bae iumi finis wetem trifala hapi sia.
Merry Christmas!	Hapi Krismas!
Our first speaker is (Chief David).	Mekwan spika blong iumi hemi (Sif Daviti).

TIME & DATES

In past centuries, the people of the Solomon Islands had traditional ways of telling time and dates which varied from one island to another. The common ways of determining them were by the movement of the sun and moon and the direction of the wind. From sunrise to sunset they would usually distinguish morning, middle of the day, and evening. There were no clocks or watches until sailors and missionaries came to the islands. Months were determined by the appearance of the new moon, and shorter periods by the phases of the moon which are important for fishing. Seasons could be told by the change in the direction of the wind.

Pijin terminology for time, days of the week and months of the year have all been adopted from English.

Precise time is not a concern of most Solomon Islanders, hence frequent comments about Solomon taem and waetman taem, that is, 'Solomon time' and 'white man time'. Don't get antsy or annoyed if things don't happen on time, but be at the airport on time or you may lose your seat.

Time

minute	minit
hour	aoa
day	dei
week	wik
fortnight	fotnaet
month	manis
year	iia
dusk	sapa

morning	mone/moning
noon	melewan dei
afternoon	aftanun
evening	ivining
night	naet
midnight	melewan naet

Days

What day is it today?	?Hemi wat dei nao tude?

It's ...	Hemi ...
Sunday	Sande
Monday	Mande
Tuesday	Tiusde
Wednesday	Wenesde
Thursday	Tosde
Friday	Fraede
Saturday	Satade/Sarere

Months

January	Januare
February	Febuare
March	Mas
April	Eprol
May	Mei
June	Jun
July	Julae
August	Ogus
September	Septemba
October	Oktoba
November	Novemba
December	Disemba
It's (the 24th)	Hemi (numba tuenti foa)

Telling Time

Like the 'it's' in English, hemi in the Pijin response phrases below is optional.

What time is it?	?Hemi wataem nao ia?
It's ...	Hemi ...

one o'clock	wan klok
almost one o'clock	kolsap wan klok
half past two	haf pas tu klok/haf pas tu
twenty past three	tuenti minit lusim tri klok (some radio announcers use ranawe from instead of lusim)
quarter past four	fiftin minit lusim foa
twenty to three	tuenti minit goap fo tri
quarter to four	fiftin minit goap fo foa

Useful Words

The expression distaem nao is the way to refer to right now. The word nao alone never means now except as a sentence initial conjunctions (see page 64).

formerly	long bifoa kam
now	distaem nao
later	bihaen
this morning	tude moning
this evening	tude ivining
tonight	tunaet
last night	lasnaet
tomorrow night	tumoro naet
yesterday	iestade/astade
today	tude
tomorrow	tumoro
day before yesterday	las astade
day after tomorrow	nekes tumoro
this	disfala
last	las
next	nekes

SOLOMON ISLANDS PIJIN

Seasons

Only two seasons are generally recognised in the Solomon Islands, dry and wet. However many people are aware of the four seasons

of more temperate climates and will recognize the standard
English terms spring, summer, autumn, and winter.

dry season	drae taem; taem blong san
wet season	tuwet taem; taem blong ren
south-east wind	ara
north-west wind	komburu
cyclone	saeklon
storm	stom/komburu

NUMBERS & AMOUNTS
The English numbering system has been adopted throughout in Pijin.

Cardinal numbers
The suffix -fala is usually added to numbers when used to refer to
specific items, but is most common with numbers which aren't
complex (1-20, 30, 40, 100). The suffix -fala (see page 58) is
given in the list for 1-12 only. It isn't used with dollars.

How many books do you have?	?Haomas buk nao iu garem?
I have two books.	Mi garem tufala buk.
How much is your pineapple?	?Haomas nao paenapol blong iu?
Four dollars.	Foa dola nomoa.

0	siro	9	naen/naenfala
1	wan/wanfala	10	ten/tenfala
2	tu/tufala	11	leven/levenfala
3	tri/trifala	12	tuel/tuelfala
4	foa/fofala	13	tetin/totin
5	faev/faefala	14	fotin
6	sikis/sikisfala	15	fiftin
7	seven/sevenfala	16	sikistin
8	eit/eitfala	17	seventin

18	eitin	70	seventi
19	naentin	80	eiti
20	tuenti/tuande	90	naenti
30	teti/toti	100	(wan) handred
40	foti	1000	(wan) taosen
50	fifti	100,000	(wan) handred taosen
60	sikisti	1,000,000	(wan) milion

All other numbers can be made by simple juxtaposition of the numbers.

1550 wan taosen faev handred fifti

Ordinal Numbers

Except for optional forms for first and second, all ordinal numbers are formed by adding the prefix mek- to the cardinal numbers.

1st	mekwan/faswan/fas
2nd	mektu/sekon
3rd	mektri
last one	laswan

Fractions

Fractions are not widely used. Even haf can mean simply 'part of'. One can specify by using phrases such as wanfala haf long tri, meaning 'one half in three', for 1/3.

a quarter	(wan) kuota
a third	(wan) ted
a half	(wan) haf
less than half	smolfala haf
more than half	bikfala haf
little bit	lelebet
few	lelebet
plenty	plande/staka
Enough!	!Naf nao!

EMERGENCIES

Help me!	!Iu mas helpem mi!
Call the police.	Ringim polis fo mi.
Where's the hospital/ clinic?	?Wea now hospitol/klinik?
Is there a telephone near here?	?Waswe, eni telefon kolsaplong hia?

Tok Pisin

TOK PISIN

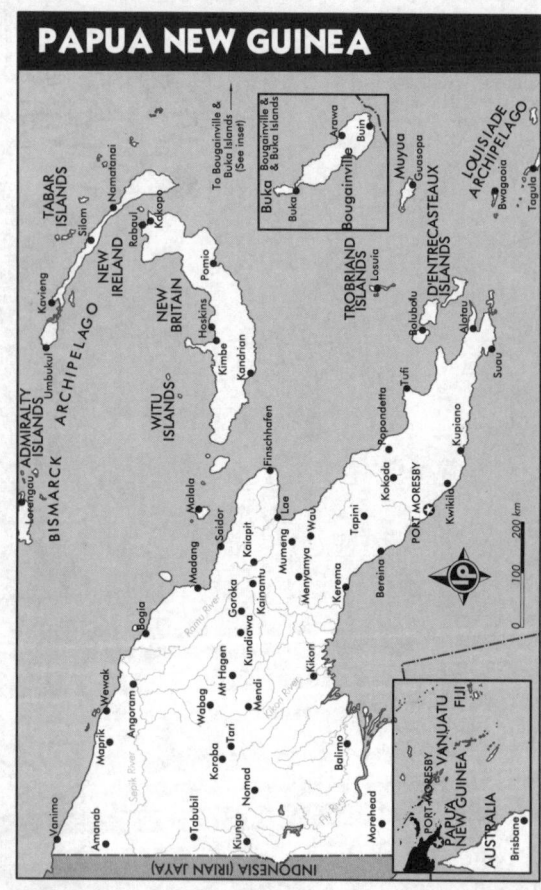

PAPUA NEW GUINEA

INTRODUCTION

Tok Pisin (or as it has also been called, New Guinea Pidgin English, Tok Boi, Neo-Melanesian) has its origins in the Pacific labour trade. Between 1880 and 1914, thousands of New Guineans worked for periods of three years or more on the German plantations of Samoa, where Pidgin English had developed as the working language of a multicultural and multilingual workforce. On returning to New Guinea, they took with them knowledge of this language. Pidgin English also became the language of the plantations the Germans established in coastal New Guinea and the islands of the Bismarck Archipelago, where young men from the more remote interior and the highlands were employed. Until very recently, the majority of Tok Pisin speakers had acquired their knowledge of the language as part of their work experience away from their home village.

Tok Pisin has grown into a language with many functions, and is now learned as a second language in most villages. For a growing number of children in the big towns, it has become creolised (adopted as their first language). The simple plantation

APPROPRIATE USE

In the colonial past, Pidgin English was used to 'talk down' to the locals and many Papua New Guineans prefer to be addressed in English rather than in bad Tok Pisin by visitors. It's advisable to negotiate whether it is appropriate to use Tok Pisin, particularly in urban areas and on formal occasions. The habit of expatriates to speak randomly simplified English, interspersed with a few Tok Pisin words, was widespread in colonial days. This variety of speech is referred to as Tok Masta, 'language of the white man', and is not acceptable to Papua New Guineans.

language of the 1920s and 1930s has changed into the national language of independent Papua New Guinea, and as such is used regularly by more than two million speakers, not only in former German New Guinea, but also in former Papua.

The spread of Tok Pisin is due not so much to deliberate policies (in fact both the German and Australian governments opposed its use for quite some time), but its perceived usefulness as a common language in a country where more than 800 languages are spoken. Tok Pisin is the major lingua franca of PNG, and it's rare even in very remote villages not to find someone who speaks it.

Much maligned as a broken English, bastard language or comic opera talk in colonial days, Tok Pisin is a vigorous and expressive language used in parliament, education, churches, and the media. It has been a written language since the 1920s, and although an official writing system exists (used in the Nupela Testamen and Wantok newspaper), non-standard spellings continue to be widely used. The most widely written and spoken variety of Tok Pisin is that of the Madang region.

There is relatively little regional variation in Tok Pisin (although some speakers distinguish between islands, lowlands and highlands Tok Pisin), but there is substantial difference between conservative rural varieties and anglicised urban ones. Our guide errs on the conservative side as, generally speaking, speakers of progressive urban varieties usually understand more conservative rural speakers, but not vice versa.

Tok Pisin speakers are tolerant of variation and visitors will find the language invaluable when they move away from the towns and want talk to Papua New Guineans socially.

PRONUNCIATION

Most Tok Pisin words are of English origin, but many words referring to local phenomena originate in local languages such as Tolai (spoken around Rabaul).

TOK PISIN

Only a small number of Papua New Guineans speak Tok Pisin as their first language (about 100,000) and they are mainly in towns or nontraditional settlements. Second language Tok Pisin speakers are often influenced in their pronunciation, grammar, and language use by the conventions of their mother tongue.

Vowels & Diphthongs

Tok Pisin and diphthongs are pronounced clearly as in Italian or German, even in an unstressed position and at the end of a word.

a   as the 'a' in 'art'
e   as the 'e' in 'set'
i   as the 'i' in 'sit'
o   as the 'o' in 'lot'
u   as the 'u' in 'put'

ai as the 'i' in 'time'
au as the 'ou' in 'house'
oi as the 'oi' in 'boil'

Consonants

Most of Tok Pisin's consonants are pronounced as in English, however some English consonants such as 'th', 'sh', 'ch' do not occur. Thus ship becomes sip. Also there's rarely a distinction between 'f and 'p' in Tok Pisin.

fire	paia
pump/palm	pam

Many speakers omit h at the beginning of words.

how much/many	amas/hamas
seat/origin/reason/cause/arse	as/has

Consonant clusters are rare in Tok Pisin. Clusters in words borrowed from English are avoided by:

Inserting Vowels	
stone	siton
spear	supia

Omitting Consonants	
station/plantation	tesen
hand	han

Outside urban areas pronunciation may vary from the standard to more closely reflect that of local languages.

English	Standard	Nonstandard
tobacco	tabak	tambak
to look/see	lukim	rukim
stone/rock/pebble	ston/siton	ton
something of mine; my genitals	samting bilong mi	satin bolo mi

GRAMMAR

In common with other pidgin languages, the grammar of Tok Pisin is relatively simple, but not an ad hoc simplification of English.

Word Order

The basic word order for all sentences is subject+verb+object. The verb and object (predicate) are introduced by the little particle i. The predicate can be:

A Verb	
The car was speeding.	Kar i hariap.
The crocodile saw the hunter.	Pukpuk i lukim sutman.

TOK PISIN

An Adjective

The bank is big.   Haus mani i bikpela.

Articles

In Tok Pisin the definite article 'the' does not exist. The indefinite article 'a', can be optionally expressed by wanpela.

a/the dog(s)   dok
a dog   wanpela dok

Definite pronouns can be expressed by dispela + noun, or noun + ya.

this village   dispela ples; ples ya

Nouns

There is no grammatical gender in Tok Pisin, but sex differences are indicated by adding man 'male' or meri 'female' after a noun.

boar	pik man	mare	hos meri
sow	pik meri	boy/son	pikinini man
stallion	hos man	girl/daughter	pikinini meri

Plurals

Distinguishing number is optional, particularly where the context makes it clear that you're dealing with two or more entities. Number can be distinguished when needed for clarity.

pig/pigs   pik
two pigs   tupela pik
pigs (pl)   ol pik
lots of pigs   plenti pik
some pigs   sampela pik

The plural marker ol is most common with nouns referring to people or larger animals.

people	ol manmeri
horses	ol hos

Smaller animals don't normally take ol.

insects; creepy crawlies	binatang

Pronouns

Singular		
1st person	I/me	mi
2nd person	you	yu
3rd person	he/she/it/him/her	em
	it (as an object in a sentence)	en
Plural		
1st person exclusive	we/us	mipela
1st person inclusive	we/us	yumi
2nd person	you (plural)	yupela
3rd person	they/them	ol

When the the pronouns mi 'I/me' and yu 'you'(sg) are the subject of a sentence, the predicate marker i is typically omitted.

I'm going.	Mi go.
He/She is going.	Em i go.

When the relationship between possessor and possessed is reciprocal or if the possesed is part of a larger whole (body parts for instance), bilong + possessor becomes obligatory.

He saw a woman.	Em i lukim meri.
He saw his wife.	Em i lukim meri bilong en.

After long and bilong, em becomes en.

Verbs

Transitive Marker

Verbs which have an object (transitive verbs) are distinguished formally from verbs which do not (intransitive verbs), by the addition of -im. Compare:

TOK PISIN

to speed	hariap	to speed something up	hariapim
to be outside	raus	to throw out	rausim
to boil	boil	to boil something	boilim

Tense

Events that will take place in the future can optionally be signalled by baimbai/bai before the verb. Events that have taken place in the past can be optionally marked by bin before the verb or pinis after it. Context and time adverbials are often sufficient to make it clear which tense you're referring to. Verbs that aren't marked can refer to any tense.

It will rain.	Baimbai/Bai ren i pundaun. (lit: the rain will fall down)
I shall return.	Bai mi kam bek/Mi bai kam bek.
The rain has fallen/It rained.	Ren i pundaun pinis.

Baimbai usually expresses a greater degree of tentativeness than bai.

The banana(s) will eventually be ripe.	Baimbai banana i mau.
If you get drunk, your wife will be cross.	Sapos yu spak meri bilong yu bai kros.

A completed action is indicated by bin or pinis.

I saw the dog over there.	Mi bin lukim dok long hap.

However the marker pinis can change the sense or meaning of a word. Note the following:

I am looking for my purse.	Mi painim hanpaus bilong mi.
I found my purse.	Mi painim pinis hanpaus.
The water is heating.	Wara i boil.
The water is boiling.	Wara i boil pinis.
The patient is unconscious.	Sikman i dai.
The patient is dead.	Sikman i dai pinis.

There's no equivalent to the English '-ing' (progressive) forms, but continuous actions are sometimes indicated by means of wok long 'be doing' or i stap 'be in state'. The latter option is favoured with adjectives and passive verbs.

He/She is (busy) cleaning the kitchen.	Em i woklong klinim haus kuk.
He was imprisoned for some time.	Em i kalabus i stap.

Direction Verbs

In a rugged country like Papua New Guinea with few roads and road signs, talking about space and directions is very important. Some local languages have elaborate systems to mark direction. Tok Pisin has only two: i kam signalling movement towards the speaker, and i go signalling movement away from the speaker.

Bring the food (to the speaker).	Yu karim kaikai i kam; Yu karim i kam kaikai.
Take the food away (from the speaker).	Yu karim kaikai i go; Yu karim i go kaikai.

Reduplication & Repetition of Verbs

Verbs or parts of verbs may be repeated to indicate intensity of action, involvement of many participants or long duration.

The old man hit the dog.	Lapun ya i paitim dok.
The old man hit the dog severely/many times.	Lapun ya i paitpaitim dok.
The women hid in the jungle.	Ol meri i hait long bus.
The women hid all over the jungle.	Ol meri i haithait long bus.

Some verbs are always reduplicated but with no special meaning.

to eat	kaikai
to dance/celebrate	singsing
to think	tingting

Adjectives

Tok Pisin has far fewer adjectives than English, and the difference between adjective and intransitive verb is often blurred. True adjectives tend to refer to external qualities.

big	bikpela
black	blakpela
long	longpela
huge	draipela
small	smolpela

Adjectives with one syllable typically take the ending -pela when placed before a noun.

Sago is good food.	Saksak i *gutpela* kaikai.
A huge wind capsized the canoe.	*Draipela* win i kapsaitim kanu.

When used predicatively (following the predicate marker i like an intransitive verb), the -pela is often dropped.

a big tree	bikpela diwai
The tree is big.	Diwai i bik(pela).
a short road	sotpela rot
The road is short.	Rot i sot(pela).

Adjectives with two or more syllables tend not to take the -pela affix.

a small lake	liklik raunwara
an old woman	lapun meri

Finally, a few frequently used adjectives follow the noun.

A bad man stole the car.	Man *nogut* i stilim kar.
The children like ripe bananas a lot.	Ol pikinini laikim tumas banana *mau*.

TOK PISIN

Nating after adjectives, verbs and nouns expresses a sense of uselessness, futility, being very ordinary or somehow undesirable.

This man is just tall (has no other distinguishing features).	Man ya i longpela nating.
an unimportant person	man nating
to sit around for no particular purpose	sindaun nating

Adverbs

Adverbs are words that modify either adjectives of verbs or whole sentences. Most Tok Pisin adjectives (usually without -pela) can also be used as adverbs.

The dog barked loudly.	Dok i singaut strong.
The child knows English well.	Pikinini i save gut Tok Inglis.

Conjunctions

Phrases and sentences can be joined by the conjunctions na 'and', o 'or', and tasol 'but'.

coast and highlands	nambis na hailans
big or little snakes/worms	bikpela o liklik snek
I arrived and I had a bath.	Mi kamap na mi go waswas.
I want to go but I have no money.	Mi laik go tasol mi no gat mani.

There are only a few other widely used conjunctions in Tok Pisin and they are not commonly used by older speakers. The main ones are taim 'when' and bikos/long wanem 'because'.

When the sun goes down there is a big feast.	Taim san i go daun i gat bikpela singsing.
I did not come because I was sick.	Mi no kam bikos mi sik.

TOK PISIN

CONJUNCTIONS

Tok Pisin speakers are aware that there is variation in their language, and they often cater for this by using alternative expressions joined by o, 'or', as in:

| I am happy. | Mi amamas o hepi. |
| Have you got a little tobacco? | Yu gat liklik tabak o brus? |

Relative Sentences

Tok Pisin has several ways of expressing relative sentences.

- The relative pronoun we 'who/which/where'.

| We went down to the river where there were crocodiles (in it). | Mipela go daun long wara we pukpuk i stap longen. |
| I saw a man who walked along the road. | Mi lukim man we wokabaut long rot. |

- Bracketing the relative sentence with ya ... ya.

| I saw a man who walked along the road. | Mi lukim man ya i wokabaut long rot ya. |

Questions

Yes/no questions are formed by adding rising intonation to statements.

Do you want/like sugar?	Yu laikim suga?
Are you coming?	Yu kam?
Are you ready?	Yu redi?

Other questions are formed by means of question words at the beginning or at the end of a sentence.

Who is/was talking?	Husat i tok?
When do/did you arrive?	Wanem taim/Wataim yu kam?
What does/did the child want?	Pikinini i laikim wanem?
What is it?	Em i wanem (samting)?

YES WE HAVE NO BANANAS

Negative questions are best avoided, as Tok Pisin speakers follow either the 'yes we have no bananas' grammar of most local languages or have adopted English conventions. In any case, it is difficult to be sure what the answer to a negative question means.

Don't you want to come?	Yunolaik kam?
No.	Yes.
Aren't you tired?	Yu no tait?
Yes I am.	Nogat.

Using Don't

The English 'don't' or 'let not' are rendered in Tok Pisin by nogut followed by a sentence with normal word order.

Don't come late.	Nogut yu kam bihain.
Don't let the pigs ruin the cemetery.	Nogut pik i bagarapim ples matamat.
I don't want to tell a lie.	Nogut mi giaman.
	(Often said when one is not sure or doesn't want to commit oneself.)

Prepositions

Tok Pisin has only two main prepositions:

Bilong, to indicate possession.

shark's tooth/teeth	tit bilong sak
my mother	mama bilong mi

Long, for most other spatial or temporal relations.

He/She went to church.	Em i go long lotu.
He/She arrived at 3 o'clock.	Em i kamap long tri klok.

Sometimes long is used instead of -im to indicate that one is dealing with a transitive verb.

I am afraid of you.	Mi pret long yu; Mi pretim yu.
You told me.	Yu tok long mi; Yu tokim mi.

FALSE FRIENDS

Most words derived from English have a similar, but seldom identical, meaning in Tok Pisin. Some words have undergone major changes in meaning. They should be carefully noted.

buttocks/seat/origin/ foundation	as
perhaps	ating (seldom 'I think', which is usually mi tingting olsem)
tired/damaged	bagarap
decorations/adornments	bilas (from 'flash')
to seduce	duim
to climb; have sexual intercourse	goap/kwap
European type goods or possessions	kago
cards; good luck	kas
to hit	kilim (but kilim i dai 'to kill')
forehead	pas (seldom 'face')
passenger/tourist/freeloader	pasindia
play; have sexual relations	pilai
to have illicit sexual relations	pilai nogut
poor/worthless	rabis

MEETING PEOPLE

As you travel around Papua New Guinea you'll be impressed with the friendliness and outgoing nature of the people. Unlike some Western countries, people in Papua New Guinea will want to greet you and talk with you, whether you know them or not. This does not apply as much to women as, by tradition, Papua New Guinean women are discouraged from speaking to strangers.

Some of the better places to meet people include markets and hotels. For women, the child clinics offer good opportunities to meet nurses, who in turn may introduce you to their friends and family.

Be aware of 'obligation networks', which involve sharing food and drink with friends.

BODY LANGUAGE

Tok Pisin is a language that 'unites' people from over 800 different cultures. As a result, speakers will generally use the body language appropriate to their local culture. When going from region to region it's best to be sensitive to variations and whenever possible to ask a local. For instance, in some regions it's considered rude to look women in the face but in others it's accepted. Having said this, one nonverbal practice that's increasingly common across the country is handshaking.

Greetings & Civilities

Hello.	Gude.
Good morning.	Moning.
Good afternoon.	Apinun.
How are you?	Yu stap gut?
I'm well.	Mi stap gut.
Please sit down.	Yu laik i sin daun.
Excuse me.	Sori.

TOK PISIN

Thank you.	Tenkyu.
Thank you very much.	Tenkyu tru.
Goodbye.	Lukim yu.

WHO IS YOUR NAME?

Names are regarded as part of a person by many Papua New Guineans. This is reflected in the use of the question word husat 'who' as in:

| What is your name? | Husat nem bilong yu?
(lit: Who is your name?) |

In many remote parts of the country it is not polite to ask a person's name directly. If in doubt, address people as wantok 'friend', lapun 'old man', or such like.

Small Talk

My name is ...	Nem bilong mi ...
I'm pleased to meet you.	Mi amamas long mitim yu.
I don't understand.	Mi no save.
More slowly please.	Yu tok isi isi plis.
May I take a photo of you?	Inap mi kisim poto bilong yu?
Is it OK or not?	I orait o nogat?

Photography is not universally welcomed and great care should be taken to ask permission to photograph people, sacred objects, and sacred buildings or sites. Take the address of people and send them pictures – they'll appreciate it. Although the government doesn't encourage payment for photography, it's often expected.

Age

| How old are you? | Hamas krismas; yias bilong yu? |
| I'm ... years old. | Mi gat ... krismas/yias. |

TOK PISIN

Nationality

You'll find that many country names in Tok Pisin are very similar to English. If your country is not listed below try saying it in English and you'll most likely be understood.

Where are you from?   Ples bilong yu we?

I'm from ...   Ples bilong mi ...
  Africa   Aprika
  Australia   Ostrelya
  Britain   Inglan
  Canada   Kanada
  Europe   Yurop
  France   Franis/Ples bilong ol man wiwi
  Germany   Jermani/Siamani
  Holland   Holan
  Japan   Siapan
  New Zealand   Niu Silan
  Solomon Islands   Solomon Ailan
  the USA   Amerika

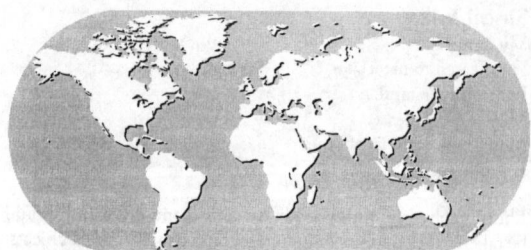

Occupations

What's your job?   Wanim kain wok bilong yu?

I'm a/an ...   Mi ...
  agricultural worker   didiman
  bartender   man;meri i lukautim haus drink
  builder   kapenta

TOK PISIN

bus driver	man bilong draivim bas; basdraiwa
doctor	dokta
engineer	insinia
farmer	man i wokim gaden; pama
fisherman	man i hukim pis
journalist	man;meri i raitim ol stori (i go) long niuspepa
mechanic	mekanik
missionary	misin/misinari
musician	man bilong pilai long stringben
nun	sista/swesta
nurse	nes
policeman	polisman/sutman
priest	pater
researcher	man;meri i painimaut ol kainkain save
shopkeeper	stuaman/stuameri/stuakipa
soldier	soldia
student	studen/sumatin
taxi driver	teksi draiwa
teacher	tisa
tourist	turis/pasindiaman/meri
waiter	weta

I'm unemployed.   Mi no gat wok.

Religion

What's your religion?   Yu bilong wanem lotu?

I'm ...   Mi ...
Catholic	Katolik/Popi
Christian	Kristen
Jehovah's Witness	Witnes
Lutheran	Luteran
Methodist	Metodis
Mormon	Mormon
Seventh Day Adventist	Sevende
of a traditional religion	lotu bilong tumbuna
not religious	no gat lotu; lotu nating

TOK PISIN

Family

Papua New Guinean family relationships can be very confusing to an outsider. If someone introduces you to their papa, they may not mean their paternal father but their father's brother. If you want to know if a relationship is a direct nuclear-family relationship as Europeans understand, you'll need to ask if the papa is papa tru, or in the case of a person's mother, mama tru.

If a person is asked the names of relatives, including in-laws, they'll most probably call them papa, susa, tambu for example, or even a totally fictitious name, in order to avoid using the real name, which is believed to be magic.

Are you married?	Yu marit (o nogat)?
I'm not married.	Mi no marit.
I'm single.	Mi singel/sikelman.
Do you have any children?	Yu gat pikinini?
I don't have any children.	Mi no gat pikinini.
Do you have brothers or sisters?	Yu gat bratasusa (bilong yu)?
Do you have a boyfriend/ girlfriend?	Yu gat boipren/gelpren (bilong yu)?

mother	mama
father	papa
child (girl)	pikinini meri
child (boy)	pikinini man
brother	brata
sister	susa
husband	man bilong mi/em/yu
wife	meri bilong mi/em/yu
in-laws	tambu
aunt (maternal)	kandere
aunt (paternal)	smolmama
uncle (maternal)	kandere/ankel
uncle (paternal)	smolpapa/ankel
grandfather/grandmother/ grandchild/ancestor	tumbuna
cousin	kasen

family (extended)	lain
family (nuclear)	famili
friend	pren/poroman
spirit	masalai

In many anglicised varieties of Tok Pisin, brata 'brother' and susa/sista 'sister', mean the same as in English. Similarly, ankel 'uncle' has replaced the terms smolpapa and kandere

Feelings

I'm ...	Mi ...
angry	kros
cold	kol
drunk	spak
(very) happy	amamas (tru)
hot	hat
hungry	hangre
in a hurry	mas hariap
sated	pulap
scared	pret
(very) sorry	sori (tumas)
tired	les
well	stap gut
worried	gat wari

Letter Writing

Much business in Papua New Guinea is carried out in English, as is most letter writing. Tok Pisin is the language of small businesses, such as village trade stores or cooperative societies, as well as for informal negotiations at all levels. Most Papua New Guineans haven't been formally taught the standard Tok Pisin spelling system, and business announcements and advertising continue to be written in nonstandard ways.

The expression bisnis has many meanings and connotations.

a relative of mine	bisnis bilong mi
The cargo cult activity can proceed.	Bisnis i op.

CARGO CULTS

The central theme of cargo cults is that cargo is not manufactured but produced by magic or brought to Papua New Guinea by returning dead ancestors. The belief that European goods could be obtained by a magic formula or ritual was widespread until the 1970s. The term muvmen refers to the movement of people from the interior to the coast, usually as part of a cargo movement.

GETTING AROUND

Regrettably, towns are no longer very safe places in Papua New Guinea and it's essential to take local advice on how to protect yourself. Be sensible, don't take risks, and avoid dubious company. Try to network and make friends among different groups.

Town life is in a marked contrast to village life. High rise buildings, modern hotels, restaurants, taxis, supermarkets and, of course, electricity define the centre. Extended shanty towns are found at the periphery of the larger towns. The inhabitants often have only weak links with their traditional villages, and their main and even only language tends to be Tok Pisin. High-security precincts exist for affluent town dwellers.

The dominant language of modern town life is English. For an outsider, addressing a Papua New Guinean in Tok Pisin might be considered condescending, especially if it is the Tok Masta variety (see page 99). Public servants will speak very good English, and the fluency of English spoken around Papua New Guinea is steadily improving.

Finding Your Way

What street is this?	Wanem nem bilong rot?
Can you give me directions to ...?	Inap yu soim mi rot i go long ...?

TOK PISIN

I'm looking for ...	Mi painim ...
Can I walk there?	Inap mi wokabaut long lek?
Is there transport available?	I gat bas, teksi samting?
Can you draw a map?	Inap yu wokim/droim map?
How far is it?	Em i longwe o nogat?

Where's a/the ...?	... i stap we?
airplane	balus
airport	ples balus
beach	nambis
boat	bot
bus	bas
bus stop	bas stop
church	haus lotu
hospital	haus sik
market	maket/bung
mission	misin/tesin
museum	musium
PMV(Passenger Motor Vehicle)	pi-em-vi
police station	polis stesin
school	skul
taxi	taksi/teksi

PMV – LICENSED TO CARRY

PMVs, or Passenger Motor Vehicles, can be any of a number of vehicles from utilities, tray tops to trucks, that are licensed to carry passengers – pasindia , as well as goods. They are a relatively cheap and common form of transport.

Buying a Ticket

I'd like a ... ticket to ...	Mi laik baim tiket long ...
one-way	i go long tasol
return	go na i kambek
How much is it to ... ?	Em i haumas long ...?

What time does the next ... leave?	Long wanem taim neks ... i go?
Where does the ... leave from?	... i kirap long wanem ples?
How long is the journey?	Hamas taim long go long ... ?
What time does the ... arrive?	Wanem taim ... i kamap?

Due to the country's geography, many places in Papua New Guinea have airfields. Usually the luggage and the passengers are weighed, so it's advisable to travel as light as possible. Planes are often over-booked, so expect delays and cancellations.

Make absolutely sure you can get a confirmed return flight, as it's easier to get away from a big place than return to it.

Directions

turn left	tanim lep
turn right	tanim rait
straight ahead	stret
east	is
west	wes
north	not
south	saut

up	antap
down	daun
near	klostu
far	longwe
in the middle	long namel
inside	insait
outside	ausait
behind	bihain long
in front of	ai bilong
next to	klostu long
point to	poinim/soim
there	long hap
walk	wokabaut

ARE WE THERE YET?

A Papua New Guinean's concept of distance can be very different to a European's. You may be told that something is klostu liklik 'fairly near' and find that you are still walking hours later.

FOOD

Traditional Papua New Guinean dishes are rarely palatable for travellers, and at times (especially with pork dishes) can be detrimental to those unaccustomed to them. Dishes worth trying however include: mumu (meat prepared in an earthoven), saksak (sago) and hatwara (a broth or stew combining many ingredients).

breakfast	kaikai bilong moningtaim
lunch	kaikai long belo
dinner	kaikai long nait
dessert	switkai

Eating Out

Is the restaurant open/closed?	Haus kaikai i op/pas?
What time do you open?	Wanem taim yu save opim haus kaikai?

Can I see the menu please?	Inap mi lukim pas bilong ol kaikai/menyu plis?
Do you have an English menu?	Yu gat pas bilong ol kaikai/menyu long Tok Inglis?
Table for ... please.	Yu gat tebol long ... manmeri plis?
Does this dish have meat?	I gat abus long dispela kaikai?
I don't eat beef/pork/chicken/dairy products.	Mi tambu long bulmakau/pik/kakaruk/susu samting.
I'm hungry.	Mi hangre.
I'm thirsty.	Nek bilong mi i drai.
I'd like ...	Mi laikim ...
Excuse me waiter.	Sori weta.
Can you bring me ...	Inap yu kisim i kam ...
The bill please.	Mi laik peim kaikai bilong mi.
I enjoyed the meal.	Mi laikim tumas dispela kaikai.

Meat

beef	bulmakau
chicken	kakaruk
duck	pato
goat	meme
lamb	sipsip
meat	abus
pork	pik
sausage	sosis

Seafood

crab	kuka
crayfish	kindam
fish	pis
octopus	kurita
oyster	kina/wusta
prawn	liklik kindam
shark	sak
squid	tauka

TOK PISIN

aiskrim
bia
kokonas

Vegetables

asparagus	pitpit (bilong waitman); asparagus
bean	bin/bonen
breadfruit	kapiak
cabbage	kapis
carrot	karot
cucumber	kukumba/guruken
ginger	kawawar
onion	anian
pandanus	karuka/marita
peas	hebsen/pis
sago	saksak
sweet potato	kaukau
tapioca	tapiok
taro	taro
tomato	tomato
vegetables	sayor/kumu/kumis
yam	yam

TOK PISIN

Fruit

banana	banana
coconut (green)	kulau
coconut (ripe)	kokonas
guava	guava
lemon	muli (i gat pait)
orange	switmuli
Malay apple	laulau
mango	mango
pineapple	painap/nanas
pawpaw	popo

Dairy

butter	bata
cheese	sis
cream	strongpela susu
ice cream	aiskrim
milk	susu

Eggs

egg	kiau
boiled/fried eggs	kiau ol i boilim/praiim

Breads & Cereals

biscuits	biskit
bread	bret
cake	kek
flour	plaua
pancake	penkek
rice	rais
toast	tos

Cooking Methods

cook/to cook	kuk/kukim
fry/to fry	prai/praiim
steam/to steam	mumu/mumuim
to boil	boilim
to prepare a meal	rediim kaikai
to roast	praiim

Drinks

alcohol	wiski
beer	bia
black coffee	kopi i blak/ret
drink/to drink	dring/dringim
orange juice	muliwara
soft drink	loli wara
tea	ti
water	wara
white coffee	kopi wantaim susu
wine	wain

Useful Words

ashtray	sitdis; plet bilong putim sit bilong smok
to eat	kaikaim
food	kaikai
fork	pork
fresh	nupela
hot	hat
knife	naip
pepper	pepa
plate	plet
ripe	mau
salt	sol
spoon	spun
stale	nogut
sugar	suga
sweet	swit
teaspoon	liklik spun

SHOPPING
At the Market

You are likely to spend some of your time shopping in the public markets of the bigger towns where a profusion of food items, artefacts and utensils are offered. Prices are usually indicated and aren't particularly flexible. If an item appears overpriced try:

Are you willing to sell it for less?   I gat seken prais?

Smaller towns have a ples bung 'village market' or a tret stua 'trade store'. Don't expect to find much variety or any sophisticated goods. Also, do not step over the goods displayed on the ground as this is tambu – it is believed that they'll spoil.

DID YOU KNOW ...	A bilum or string bag is made from natural fibres. Each village has its own design, and Papua New Guineans will often be able to tell you where you got yours. Young babies are carried in bilum(s) by their mothers, which may be the reason for the second meaning of bilum, 'womb'.

The tourists would like to buy something.	Turis i laik baim sampela samting.
What's that?	Wanem dispela?
How much is it?	Hamas long dispela?
How many/much?	Hamas?
The price is too steep.	Pe i antap tumas.
That's very cheap.	Pe/Prais i daun (tru).
I'm just looking.	Mi lukluk tasol.
Where can I get/find ...?	Mi ken (i) kisim/painim we ...?

TOK PISIN

I'd like to buy ...	Mi laik baim ...
a carving	kaving/imis
this stringbag	dispela bilum

This is a really nice stringbag.	Yes, gutpela bilum tru.
Do you wish to buy it or not?	Yu laik baim o nogat?
I'll take/have it.	Bai mi kisim.
That one.	Dispela (ya).

Is it ...?	Em i ...?
sweet	switpela
sour	i (gat) pait
fresh	nupela

SIGNS

NO KEN DINAU.
NO CREDIT.

EM KRISTEN STUA. I NOGAT DRINK, SMOK SAMTING.
THIS IS A CHRISTIAN STORE. WE DO NOT STOCK DRINK OR TOBACCO PRODUCTS.

TAMBU LONG KAIKAI BUAI.
IT IS PROHIBITED TO CHEW BETELNUT.

Village Trade Stores

The range of goods available from village trade stores is very limited. Usually you will find:

batteries	ol batari
bra	kalabus bilong susu
	(lit: prison for breasts).
assorted cigarettes	kainkain smok
fishhooks	huk
jumper	kolsiot (lit: cold shirt)
kerosene	kerosin
matches	masis
needles	nil
newspaper to roll your own	smokpepa

TOK PISIN

singlet	singlis
(scented) soap	(smel)sop
underpants	andapens
washing powder	soppaura

ACCOMMODATION
Checking In

Do you have a single room?	Yu gat rum slip long wanpela man/meri tasol?
Do you have a double room?	Yu gat rum slip long tupela manmeri?
How much is it per night?	Em i kostim hamas long wanpela de?
Can I see the room?	Inap mi lukim rum pastaim?
I want to see another room.	Mi laik lukim narapela rum.
I like this room.	Mi laikim (tru) dispela rum.
Is there a cheaper room?	I gat rum i no dia tumas?
Is there a mosquito net?	I gat taunam/moskita net/ klambu i stap?
Where's the toilet?	Haus pekpek/smolhaus/toilet i stap we?
I want to stay ... day(s).	Mi laik stap ... de.
Is there a weekly rate?	Em i kostim hamas long wanpela wik?
Could I have my key please?	Inap mi ken kisim ki plis?
Any messages/letters for me?	I gat pas i kamap (bi)long mi?
My room number is ...	Namba bilong rum bilong mi i ...
Is there a ...?	I gat rum ...?
bath/shower	waswas (i stap)
laundry	bilong wasim (ol) klos
I'd like to check out today/ tomorrow.	Mi laik bai mi lusim hotel tede/tumora.

Can you call a taxi?   Inap yu kolim teksi (bi)
long mi?

Requests & Complaints

I'd like (a) ...	Mi laikim ...
bath	waswas
blanket	blanket
bucket	baket
curtains	laplap bilong windua/ketin
electricity	paua/lektrik
hot water	wara i hat
light	lam
mirror	glas (bilong) lukluk
pillow	pilo
big room	rum i bikpela
quiet room	rum i nogat planti nois longen
towel	laplap bilong draiim skin

It's too ...	Em i ... tumas.
big/small	bikpela/liklik
cold/hot	kolpela/hatpela
dark/dirty	tudak/doti
noisy	nois (Nois also means 'to shake/ quiver'.)

Please do not disturb.   No ken kirapim mi.
(But note that kirapim also has the
sexual connotation of 'to arouse'.)

AROUND TOWN
At the Bank

The basic unit of currency in Papua New Guinea is the kina(K).
It's made up of 100 toea(t). Coins are 1t, 2t, 5t, 10t, 20t, 50t,
and K1. Notes are K2, K5, K10, and K20. Most large towns
have one or two banks. In general, English is the preferred
language of banking.

bank	haus mani/benk
money	mani
cheque/cheque book	sek/sekbuk

I'd like to ...	Mi laik ...
change money	senisim mani
deposit money	putim mani long haus mani; subim mani long sek
withdraw money	rausim mani long haus mani
cash a cheque	senisem sek long mani

At the Post Office

I'd like a stamp.	Mi laik baim stem.
I want to send a letter/ postcard to ...	Mi laik salim pas; poskat i go long ...
How much is it?	Em i hamas?

airmail	salim pas i go long balus
envelope	paus
poste restante	pas i stap long pos opis
surface mail	surfismel

Filling Out Forms

name	nem bilong yu
address	atres bilong yu
nationality	as ples bilong yu
age	hamas krismas bilong yu
date of birth	de mama i karim yu
occupation	wanem kain wok bilong yu
signature	raitim nem bilong yu

TOK PISIN

IN THE COUNTRY

When travelling outside of towns, it's sometimes possible to stay a night or two in smaller villages. However, it's not advisable to turn up unannounced. The best approach is to go to a market in a nearby town and find some villagers from the village where you want to go. It's far better to make arrangements in advance, as the village may not have any suitable accommodation, food, or water. Before pitching a tent it's important to make sure that it's creepy crawly proof. For good reason, the better and safer village houses are on stilts.

When bushwalking, local guides are often required, as many of the tracks may be difficult to follow. Permission is needed to travel through some areas, and information can be sought in markets, from villagers and missionaries, and from local officials. Rates of pay for guides and carriers usually involve bargaining.

Huts for visiting patrol officers, haus kiap , can also provide useful short-term accommodation. They are usually very basic and unfurnished.

Can I look around the village?	Inap mi lukluk raun long ples?
Is there food/water available?	I gat kaikai/wara?
Where have you come from?	Yu stap we na yu kam?
Where are you going?	Yu go we?
Can I/we take a rest here?	Inap mi/yumi malolo liklik?
Can I sleep here?	Inap mi ken i slip long ples?
Is there a patrol officer's hut?	I gat haus kiap?

Where is the ...	... i stap we?
airfield	ples balus
canoe	kanu
government office	ofis bilong gavman
lake	raunwara
mission	misin/stesin
mountain	maunten
resting place	ples bilong malolo
river	wara
road/trail	rot
village	ples

TOK PISIN

What's the name of this ... ?	Yu kolim wanem (nem) dispela ... ?
animal	abus
bird	pisin
flower	plaua
tree	diwai

Animals & Birds

ants	anis
bird	pisin
bird of paradise	kumul
bull/cow	bulmakau
cassowary	muruk
cat	pusi
crocodile	pukpuk
cuscus	kapul
hornbill	kokomo
insect	binatang
mosquito	natnat
pig	pik
possum	kapul
python	moran
sheep	sipsip
snake	snek

'SEND A LEAF'

Cordilyne leaves may come in many colours and shapes and fulfil numerous cultural functions. Planting cordilynes around the house keeps ghosts at bay, crossing cordilyne leaves over each other may signal taboo and prohibit entry. Sending someone the leaves can mean an invitation. Salim tanget 'send a leaf' is an old expression for sending a letter.

Useful Words

address	adres/atres
bicycle	baskol/baisikel
dangerous	nogut/tambu
here	hia
luggage	kago
map	map
mosquito net	taunam; moskita net; klambu
passport	paspot
rest	malolo
seat	sia
spirit house	haus tambaran

TOK PISIN

stop	stap
ticket	tiket
toilet	haus pekpek; smolhaus
wood/log/tree	diwai

FESTIVALS & MYTHOLOGY

You will encounter two kinds of festivals in Papua New Guinea: traditional singsing 'dances, feasts', and Christian festivals such as Christmas and Easter. Papua New Guineans are proud to display their culture to outsiders, but don't gatecrash as many festivals have deep cultural significance and may be tambu 'taboo' (like funeral ceremonies). Cultural practices vary widely, and visitors are advised to consult relevant literature for the region they plan to visit. The Tourism Promotion Authority is a good source for the dates of regional festivals that can vary from year to year.

The all-night yam festivals of the Maprik region (East Sepik Province), celebrating the harvest season, are particularly impressive, taking place against the background of the triangular haus tambaran 'spirit house'. Note that the cultivation and harvesting of yams is considered men's work and that some aspects of this festival may not be watched by women.

Other regional festivals of note include the Port Moresby Show in June, which is both a traditional singsing and an agricultural show, the Mt Hagen Show in July which sees the meeting of

Highlands clans, and the yam festival on the Trobriand Islands, also in July.

Apart from traditional Christian festivals, such as Easter, Christmas and New Year, the other main nationwide celebration is Independence Day, on 16th September.

The two central aspects of traditional mythology concern the worship of tumbuna 'ancestors' and the worship of masalai 'spirits'. In essence, nature is seen as being inhabited by tumbuna and masalai. In traditional villages stori bilong tumbuna 'stories about the ancestors or ancestral times' are very popular. Taim bilong tumbuna is a common expression for the days before white colonisation (which began around 1880) or contacts with white people. In some remote areas the first contacts were made in the late 1960s.

TIME & DATES

Traditionally, the perception of time was cyclical and not linear as in Western countries. Time was not cut up into measurable units, and even today don't expect 'punctuality' to play the same role as it does in Western societies. Villagers often feel uncomfortable with the concept of being paid by the hour rather than for a particular job.

Days

Sunday	Sande
Monday	Mande
Tuesday	Tunde
Wednesday	Trinde
Thursday	Fonde
Friday	Fraide
Saturday	Sarere

day	de
week	wik
yesterday	asde
the day before yesterday	hapasde/asde bipo

TOK PISIN

today	tede
tomorrow	tumora
the day after tomorrow	haptumora
next week	neks wik/wik bihain

Months

January	Janueri
February	Februeri
March	Mas
April	Epril
May	Me
June	Jun
July	Julai
August	Ogas
September	Septemba
October	Oktoba
November	Novemba
December	Desemba

month	mun
year	yia
next month	neks mun/mun bihain

What's the date today? Tede em i wanem de tru?
It's (the 5th) of March. Tede i (de namba faiv) bilong mun Mas.

Telling the Time

When/At what time? Wanem taim?
What time is it? Wanem taim nau?

It's ... Em i ...
    eight o'clock et klok
    five to eight faiv minut i go painim et klok
    five past eight faiv minut i go lusim et klok

    sunrise taim bilong san i kamap
    morning moningtaim
    midday belo kaikai

TOK PISIN

afternoon	apinun
sundown	taim bilong san i godaun
twilight	hapnait
evening (7 – 11)	nait
night (11 – 4)	biknait

Seasons/Weather

The seasons in Papua New Guinea are taim bilong ren 'rainy season' and taim bilong drai 'dry season'. In river areas you may hear: haiwara (lit: high river) 'rainy season' and draiwara (lit: dry river) 'dry season'.

Caution should be taken when asking about weather conditions, as Papua New Guineans will tend to tell you what they think you want to hear.

TOK PISIN

It is/will be ...	Em i/Bai em i ...
clear	taim klia
cold	kol
fine	naispela taim
hot	hat
raining	ren
sunny	san
windy	win

NUMBERS & AMOUNTS

There are many traditional counting systems in Papua New Guinea which exist alongside the modern decimal system, spread by schools and modern lifestyles.

The traditional systems range from simple binary ones (one, two, many) to decimal systems. Along with true number systems, there are many tally systems in which body parts are pointed to when counting.

Tok Pisin speakers employ either the traditional expressions listed here or English numbers (like 'eleven' for wanpela ten wan).

Counting with your fingers is typically subtractive with the little finger displayed on its own signalling 'four', two fingers signalling 'three', three fingers signalling 'two' and so on.

Different groups can have very different attitudes to numbers and counting. Do not expect precise numerical information on all occasions.

Cardinal Numbers

1	wan	11	wanpela ten wan
2	tu	12	wanpela ten tu
3	tri	13	wanpela ten tri
4	foa	14	wanpela ten foa
5	faiv	15	wanpela ten faiv
6	sikis	16	wanpela ten sikis
7	seven	17	wanpela ten seven
8	et	18	wanpela ten et
9	nain	19	wanpela ten nain
10	ten	20	tupela ten

TOK PISIN

21	tupela ten wan	80	etpela ten
22	tupela ten tu	90	nainpela ten
30	tripela ten	100	wan handet
31	tripela ten wan	101	wan handet wan
40	fopela ten	1 000	tausen
50	faivpela ten	10,000	tenpela tausen
60	sikispela ten	100,000	handetpela tausen
70	sevenpela ten	one million	wan milian

Ordinals

1st	namba wan
2nd	namba tu
3rd	namba tri

Amounts

a little	liklik	many	planti
double	dabolim	more	moa
dozen	dasan	once	wanpela
enough	inap	some	sampela
half	hap	too much	tumas
less	liklik tru	twice	tupela

EMERGENCIES

I have a little problem.	Mi gat liklik wari bilong mi.
I need help.	Mi laikim sampela halp; Mi laik yu halpim mi.
I'm in trouble.	Mi gat trabel.
What do you want?	Yu laikim wanem samting?
What's the matter?	Olsem wanem; Wasmara?
Don't worry.	No ken wori.
Shout.	Singaut.

Other Creoles

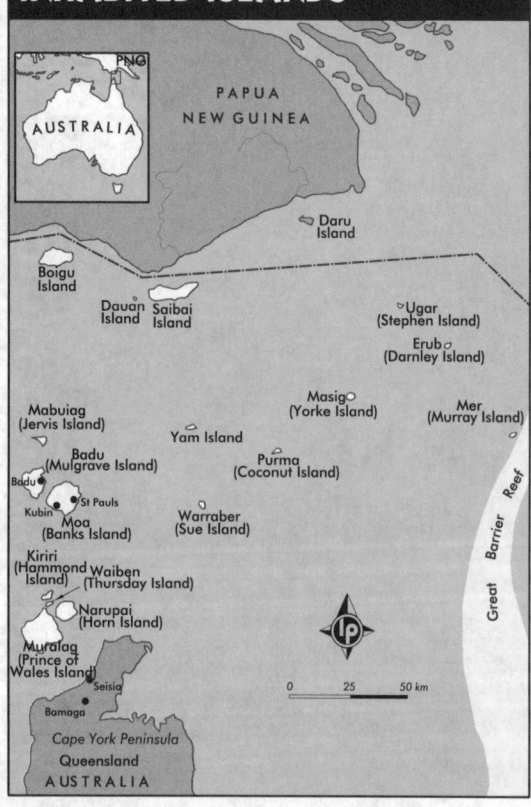

TORRES STRAIT - INHABITED ISLANDS

OTHER CREOLES OF THE REGION

YUMPLA TOK

Yumpla Tok, previously known as Torres Strait Broken, is one of three languages spoken in the region which is comprised of a group of small islands scattered along Torres Strait, between the tip of Cape York, Australia and Papua New Guinea. While Kala Lagaw Ya and Meriam Mar are the original indigenous languages and are spoken in particular regions, Yumpla Tok is an English-based creole that acts as the region's lingua franca. It's mainly spoken in the Eastern and Central Islands and Thursday Island, and is the first language of most people there who were born after WWII.

Yumpla Tok was the result of colonisation. It developed mainly from the Vanuatu pidgin, Bislama, which was brought to Torres Strait by Pacific Islanders who came to the area as labourers in the marine industry.

Interactions between Pacific Islanders, Torres Strait Islanders and other nationals who had migrated to the area, such as Japanese, Malayans and Chinese, resulted in the emergence of Yumpla Tok which is now distinctly different from Bislama as spoken today.

Out of a total population of 30,000, about 6000 Torres Strait Islanders actually live in the Torres Strait and continue to use these languages. The remaining 80% have moved to the provincial towns and cities in the mainland of Australia.

European contact has had devastating effects on the languages and culture of Torres Strait Islanders. The colonisation process and the cruel policies of assimilation, segregation and integration have greatly contributed to the marginalisation of Torres Strait Islander culture and languages. Official limitations were placed on the use of indigenous languages in schools and public places. Despite total exposure to the dominant Western culture and English language, Torres Strait Islanders on the mainland have managed exceptionally well to maintain their traditional languages. Kala

OTHER CREOLES

Lagaw Ya has about 3000 speakers, while Meriam Mir speakers are numbered close to 2000, and all Torres Strait Islanders speak Yumpla Tok regardless of where they live in Australia.

In the Torres Strait today, people use Yumpla Tok on a daily basis, although most adults maintain their traditional indigenous languages.

On the Islands

The places that are visited most frequently by outsiders are Bamaga, Seisia and Thursday Island. In winter, tourists travel by road to Cape York and camp in the camping area at Seisia. A regular ferry operates from Thursday Island, to service the Northern Peninsula Area communities, on most days of the week.

Thursday Island is the commercial and administrative centre for Torres Strait. It has a fasinating history. The fort is one of the main attractions on Thursday Island. On Green Hill there are 16 inch guns which were built at the turn of the century in fear of a Russian invasion that never eventuated. Thursday Island is surrounded by a number of islands clustered together. The airport is on Horn Island and the airlines provide regular ferry services to and from Thursday Island.

All the islands not included in the Muralag (Prince of Wales) group, including Thursday Island, are referred to as outer islands. To visit any of the outer islands, it's important to make an arrangement with the Council of the island because of limited accommodation.

Variation in Yumpla Tok

The way Eastern Islanders and Central/Western Islanders speak Yumpla Tok varies in terms of the vocabulary used, the different words being derived from their indigenous languages.

Awa, yumi go.	Uncle, let's go. (Eastern)
Awadhe, yumi go.	Uncle, let's go. (Central/Western)

OTHER CREOLES

Pronunciation
Vowels
The vowels in Yumpla Tok resemble those of English.

The simple vowels are:
- a as the 'u' in 'but'
- e as the 'e' in 'pet'
- i as the 'i' in 'bit'
- o as the 'o' in 'pot'
- u as the 'u' in 'put'

The diphthongs are:
- ei as the 'ei' in 'pay'
- ai as the 'i' in 'bite'
- oi as the 'oy' in 'toy'
- au as the 'ow' in 'now'
- eu as the 'il' in 'milk' in Cockney English – an 'iw' sound

Consonants
Yumpla Tok has the consonant sounds: b, d, g, j, k, l, m, n, p, r, s, t, w, y and z – they are pronounced as in English.

Pronouns

Singular		
1st person	I	ai
2nd person	you	yu
3rd person	he/she	em
Plural		
1st person exclusive		
we (two)		mitu
we (they & I, not you)		mipla
1st person inclusive		
we (two)		yumtu
we (we & I, not you)		yumpla
2nd person		
you (two)		yutu
you (more than two)		yupla
3rd person		
they (two)		dhemtu
they (more than two)		dhempla

Greetings & Civilities

The outer island communities are changing fairly rapidly from traditional village settings to small townships. All the islands now have modern houses, schools, medical facilities, telephones and electricity. However, in general, life on the islands runs at a notably leisurely pace. The daily activities of the people revolve around family and community affairs.

The main authorities in an island community are the community council chairperson and the councillors, the priest and the clan elders. Visitors are expected to observe cultural protocol when visiting the islands. It's therefore important to find out as much as possible beforehand.

Welcome.	Maiem.
How are you?	Wis wei (yu)?
Fine.	Orait.
Have you eaten?	U bi kaikai?
I've eaten already.	Ai bi pinis kaikai.
I haven't eaten yet.	Ai no bi kaikai.
Come inside the house!	Kam insaid hous!
Thank you.	Eso po yu.
Very good.	Prapa gud.
Goodbye.	Siyu; Yawo.
Yes.	Wa.
No.	No.

Directions & the Countryside

Is that path good?	Able gab debele eki?
Not so good.	Nole able adud gab eki.
above	antap
behind	biyain
below	andanith
beside	klustun
fire	paya
hill	il
in front	prant

path	rod
left side	lep said
right	rait
rock	ston
smoke	smok
tree	tri

People & Animals

baby	beibi
friend	pren
person	man
man	man
old man	ol man
woman	oman
old woman	ol oman

cat	pusi
dog	dog
rat	rat
snake	sneik

Food

Over the years, Torres Strait Islanders have developed a lifestyle suited to their environment. At one time they depended almost entirely on the sea for food and travel from one island to the next. On land, they cultivate crops in their gardens and domesticated animals, mainly pigs. These days not much gardening is being carried out. Torres Strait Islanders rely more and more on community stores that provide general groceries, including fresh vegetables, fruit and meat. Fish is the staple food, and is caught with handlines, nets or hand spears, and is supplemented with rice, yams, sweet potatoes and taro.

Other native foods are dugong and turtle. Using traditional methods, Torres Strait Islanders spear them with a special harpoon. Because dugong and turtle are considered a luxury, people only eat them on special occasions like weddings and tombstone unveilings.

For special occasions, Torres Strait Islanders hold traditional feasts which include dancing, singing and lots of food. Traditional food requires a lot of preparation. One of the popular traditional foods is sop-sop, a mixture of vegetables chopped into small pieces and cooked in coconut cream. In just about every feast, food is cooked in an earth oven or kap mauri. The food for kap mauri is prepared and wrapped then placed on hot stones lying on the bottom of the pit specially dug in the ground. Any kind of food may be cooked in the kap mauri including vegetables, pig, dugong, turtle and damper.

Festivals & Celebrations

In May of each year, Thursday Island hosts the Torres Strait Cultural Festival. This is designed to promote and strengthen cultural identity. The activities of the Cultural Festival include traditional dance, traditional and contemporary singing, and stalls where people sell food, handicrafts, artefacts and carvings of all description.

Tombstone unveiling is one of the important family events celebrated with a big traditional feast. It involves a lot of preparation by the family of the deceased person. The preparations include the collecting of money from each member of the family, erecting a tombstone on the grave and putting on a feast.

Torres Strait Islanders are devout Christians. Most of them are Anglicans. Some islands have smaller churches of other denominations. They worship every Sunday in churches built by themselves. Church services are normally conducted in English but most of the hymns are sung in their own languages. An important religious event that people throughout the Torres Strait celebrate on 1 July each year, is the festival of the 'Coming of the Light'. This event signifies the arrival of the missionaries of the London Missionary Society in the Torres Strait in 1871. The festival is usually celebrated with a church service followed by a re-enactment of how the people on each island greeted the missionaries. In the re-enactment, some people dress as the missionaries while others dress in warrior costumes.

Dance

The most notable cultural trait that Torres Strait Islanders on all islands have hung on to so tightly apart from their languages is

OTHER CREOLES

their traditional dance. There are different styles of traditional dance which can be performed while standing upright stamping both feet, or in a sitting position. Both forms of dancing require a lot of hand movements and jumping. The dancers usually wear special costumes, depending on what the dance is about. To perform the dances the men wear a piece of cloth called lava-lava and a singlet, while women wear specially made floral dresses. Also, the dancers equip themselves with special regalia consisting of grass skirt, headress, headbands, necklaces, arm and leg bands and models representing the subject that the dance portrays. All dances are usually accompanied by singing and the pulsating rhythm of drums.

Useful Words

church	sos/mun	God	God
Holy Spirit	Oli Gos	drum	dram
priest	pris		

Further Reading

At present, there's only one publication on Yumpla Tok. It's in a book called *Broken (Introduction to the Creole Language of the Torres Strait)* by Anna Shnukal. This is primarily a dictionary, which also contains the grammar of Yumpla Tok. As for the two indigenous languages of Torres Strait, there are a number of unpublished materials available which can be researched through libraries. There is an article on a sketched grammar, and a short word list on Kalaw Kawa Ya, published in *Languages in Australia*, edited by Suzanne Romaine. The article is by Kevin Ford & Dana Ober, and is called *A Sketch of Kalaw Kawa Ya*.

For more information about Torres Strait Islander culture and lifestyle, see *Torres Strait Islanders: Custom and Colonialism* by Jeremy Beckett, or the two books by Lindsay Wilson, *Thathilgaw Emereet Lu* and *Kerkar Lu*.

Lonely Planet's *Australian Phrasebook* also contains information on these and other indigenous Australian languages.

TOP END AUSTRALIA

Cobourg Peninsula

Oenpelli (Gunbalanya)

Darwin

Arnhem Hwy

Jabiru

KAKADU NATIONAL PARK

ARNHEM LAND

Batchelor

Adelaide River

Daly River

Pine Creek

Daly River

Numbulwar

Katherine

Mataranka

Roper Hwy

East Alligator River

Ngukurr

Roper River

Larrimah

Victoria Hwy

Victoria River

Timber Creek

Daly Waters

Carpentaria Hwy

Yarralin

Top Springs

Pigeon Hole

Stuart Hwy

Newcastle Waters

Elliott

Kalkaringi

Tablelands Hwy

AUSTRALIA

PNG

0   50   100 km

Barkly Hwy

Tennant Creek

KRIOL

Kriol is a relatively new Aboriginal language that has upwards of 20,000 speakers throughout most of the Katherine Region of the Northern Territory and the neighbouring Kimberley Region in Western Australia. The name 'Kriol' has been applied relatively recently and it hasn't yet gained widespread currency among all of its speakers.

As the name suggests, Kriol is a creole language – this means that it's a kind of 'emergency language' which has a specific origin. Kriol first arose early this century when surviving members of many decimated language groups congregated at the Roper River Mission in order to escape the brutal killings being carried out by cattle station companies in the area at that time. Many of the adults who came to the Roper River Mission were multilingual, but they were certainly not multilingual in exactly the same languages. Moreover, children had not yet developed full competence in as many languages as their parents. In this situation, the only form of language available for communication among everybody – including the English-speaking missionaries – was a pidgin that had entered the Northern Territory a few decades before with the cattle trade and had become fairly widespread. Children at the mission heard more of this pidgin than of any other language, not least because the missionaries housed them in dormitories away from their elders. The children acquired the pidgin as their first language and in doing so they created a full language which was able to meet all their communicative needs.

Due to its origins, Kriol has elements in common with traditional Aboriginal languages, with English and with other creole languages. As 'new' languages, creole languages tend to have fewer of the irregularities that occur in older languages and they also tend to convey most kinds of linguistic meaning with separate words. So for instance whereas English can use the ending '-ed' to indicate past time, Kriol always uses a separate word bin to indicate an action happened in the past. For example, bin luk means 'looked'.

What's in a Name?

The name 'Kriol' has gained some currency over recent years but the use of the name 'Kriol' is still limited. Before it came into use, the term pidgin was sometimes used and some people still refer to Kriol in this way today.

Travellers to Kriol-speaking areas should note that it isn't usually productive (let alone appropriate or respectful) to walk up to an Aboriginal person and ask 'Do you speak Kriol?' The term just isn't widely enough known as yet and, even if familiar, it does not carry a sense of status or prestige for many Aboriginal people.

Travellers should also realise that they can't usually ask a Kriol speaker what language they speak and expect the answer to be Kriol. Aboriginal people usually respond to this question with the name of the traditional language that they are affiliated to, whether they speak it fully or not. This is because, from an Aboriginal perspective, asking about language is tantamount to asking what kind of person you are. A traditional Aboriginal language is always associated with its 'country', having been put in place in the dreamtime – perhaps by creator figures or maybe by ancestral beings – and its people who inherit rights over 'country' and language through one or both of their parents.

Kriol doesn't have these same associations. It is the language that many Aboriginal people in the Top End and Kimberleys use as their everyday language of communication, but not the one they are identified by.

Pronunciation
Vowels
a	as the 'a' in 'father'
e	as the 'e' in 'bed'
i	as the 'ee' in 'week'; sometimes as the 'i' in 'bin'
o	close to the 'ou' in 'sound'; sometimes as the 'o' in 'nod'
u	as the 'u' in 'put'

Diphthongs
ai	as the 'y' in 'shy'
ei	as the 'ay' in 'say'
oi	as the 'oi' in 'noise'

Sometimes you will see the last vowel in a word repeated three times, as in wok-woook which means something like 'walked and walked'. You will hear this repetition as a significantly lengthened vowel (see page 154).

Consonants

Traditional Aboriginal languages have played a very important part in shaping Kriol sounds. Just like most traditional Aboriginal languages, Kriol doesn't distinguish between pairs of sounds like b/p, d/t, g/k, f/v, or s, z and sh .

g   as the 'g' in 'go'; *not* as the 'g' in 'page'
th   as the 'th' in 'this'; *not* as the 'th' in 'thin'
rr   a flapped 'r' sound (a bit like the rolled 'r' sounds in Scots English, Spanish or Italian)
tj   as the 'ch' in 'church'

Kriol spelling isn't standardised to the same extent as English or other European languages which have a longer history of literacy. You will find that some Kriol words can be written in a number of different ways because they have varying pronunciations.

Grammar
Nouns

Kriol uses markers to indicate number. If Kriol speakers are referring to two of something, they have to mark this with dubala (sometimes tubala). To express more than two ola , is used.

dubala gel	(the) two girls
ola biliken	(the) billycans
ola kenggurru	(the) kangaroos

The suffix -mob (or sometimes -lat) is added onto nouns – or words used with nouns – to indicate a group, so it can be used as a marker for more than two.

Mela gowin gada thadmob nathalat modiga.	We're going with those other cars.
Darwin-mob bin kaman.	The people from Darwin came.

OTHER CREOLES

Pronouns

Singular		
1st person	I, me, my, mine	ai/mi/main
2nd person	you	yu
3rd person	he, him, she, her, it	im

Plural

1st person exclusive	
we (two)	minbala
we (more than two)	melabat/mela

1st person inclusive	
we (two)	yunmi/minyu
we (more than two)	wi

2nd person	
you (two)	yunbala
you (more than two)	yumob

3rd person	
they (two)	dubala

Kriol pronouns do not distinguish gender.

| Det olmen, ai bin luk im bifo. | I have seen that man before. |
| Wanbala olguman, imin dalim mi stori. | A woman told me (the) story. |

Plural forms of pronouns in Kriol, like traditional Aboriginal languages, distinguish between two and more than two.

As in traditional Aboriginal languages, the choice of some Kriol pronoun forms depends on whether the person being addressed is included or excluded. Kriol pronouns aren't usually marked for their different cases (as in English 'he', 'him', 'his'). The first person pronouns ai, mi, main are an exception to this.

OTHER CREOLES

Ai and mi are used as the subject of a sentence.

(Mi), ai bin jidanabat la   (As for me), I was staying at
    main kemp.   my place.
Mi laithad la im.   I said to him/her.

Mi is also used for emphasis (in which case it's usually right at the
very front or the end of the sentence); as the object in a sentence;
after the prepositions la (to, at) and gada (with); in sentences that
equate one thing with another (X is Y).

Mi titja la skul.   I (am a) teacher at (the) school.

Main 'my, mine, me' is used as a possessive form as well as after
the preposition ba 'for/of'.

Yu gu gaji beig ba main.   Go and get the bag for me.

There is some variation in how Kriol speakers pronounce some
pronoun forms and also in how they use them. Dei (they) is used
mostly for subject. Some speakers use alabat (sometimes dem)
only as for object while some use alabat throughout.

Yunmi is far more common than minyu, but the occasional
speaker uses the latter form.

Kriol uses just one pronoun, mijel (sometimes also mijal,
misal), for indicating an action that was done to or by 'oneself'.
This item was originally derived from the English word 'myself',
but in Kriol mijel stands for 'myself, yourself, himself, herself'.

Im oldei gu hanting mijel.   He always goes hunting (by)
                                 himself.

Prepositions
Kriol has a smaller array of prepositions than English. Two of
them (la, ba) carry most of the load.

la (sometimes also langa) 'at/in/on/to/into/onto'

Wi bin jidan la sheid.	We sat in the shade.
Wi bin jidan la gras.	We sat on the grass.
Wi bin jidan la kemp.	We sat at home.
Imin gu la taun.	He/she went to town.

ba (sometimes also: **bla**, **blanga**) 'for' (benefit)/'of' (possession) 'about'/ 'to' (association)

| Yumob bin luk thad dog ba mela? | Did you (pl) see that dog of ours/our dog? |

The other two prepositions (gada, from) have more specific uses:

gada (sometimes also **garra**, **garrim**) with/having

| Wanbala olmen jeya gada wiska. | There's a man there with a beard. |

from (sometimes also **brom**, **burrum**, **burru**) from

| Alabat bin kaman dijei burru Darwin. | They came in this direction from Darwin. |

Verbs

Kriol indicates past tense with the marker bin before a verb. This joins up with the pronoun im imin. (see page 152)

| Minbala bin wok gada ola biliken. | The two of us walked with the billycans. |
| Imin laithad la melabat ... | He said to us ... (lit: he like that to us) |

Future tense (and also necessity) is expressed with the marker gada (or garra) before a verb. (This marker sounds the same as some of the forms of the preposition gada with).

| Yumob gada gu gada yumob matha. | You (pl) will go *with* your mother; You (pl) have to go *with* your mother. |

Kriol has some interesting tools for indicating intensity of an action or event. These can be used independently or they can be combined with each other to achieve various nuances.

If something occurs regularly or habitually, Kriol uses the marker oldei implying 'usually, habitually, always, would' (often shortened to ala). Oldei was originally derived from the English expression 'all day' – but obviously doesn't have much in common with it now!

Melabat bin oldei gu fishing en hanting.	We would go fishing and hunting; we usually went fishing and hunting.

When a lot of people are involved in something, or there is a repeated series of events, Kriol often doubles the verb.

Mela bin gula-gula gija olawei.	We were telling each other off all the way.

If something happens for an uninterrupted time span (especially when this is subsequently punctuated or terminated), Kriol speakers will often lengthen or stretch out a word as they say it. (The pitch of the lengthened word is markedly higher than the surrounding words, so it sounds almost like singing.)

Minbala bin oldei wok-w-o-o-o-k.	The two of us would keep on walking and walking.

To Be

Kriol doesn't have any one item that is directly equivalent to the English verb 'to be'. To indicate existence, the Kriol verb jidan (sometimes also sidan) 'stay, stop, sit' may be used. However, where the orientation of something is important (vertical versus horizontal) or is inherent in its nature (trees 'stand' in Kriol), Kriol always prefers the use of more specific verbs such as jendap meaning 'to stand, to be vertical'.

OTHER CREOLES

Jidan kwait!	Stay quiet, be quiet!
Mela ol jidan la kemp.	We all stop in the camp; we are all in the camp.

To express equivalence between one word and another (X is Y), Kriol just places the items to be related together with no intervening element.

Thad trubala! (lit: that true)	That is true!

Question Words

wani/wanim/wot	what
Wani tharran?	What's that?
hu	who
Hu bin ringap?	Who rang?
wijei	which way
Wijei alabat bin gu?	Which way did they go?
weya	where
Weya yu modiga?	Where's your car?
wotaim	when
Wotaim yumob bin kambek?	When did you all come back?

A Trip Through Kriol Country

Kriol is spoken from as far north as Darwin to as far south as Tennant Creek. It spreads west towards the Kimberleys and east towards Queensland. The Kriol spoken varies to some degree from region to region, particularly due to the influence of local traditional languages and exposure to English. Often traditional vocabulary is used for flora, fauna, place names, bush tucker(native foods), skin names and relationship terms. In areas that have been exposed to English, the Kriol is often 'lighter'(more like English) and Aboriginal English may also be commonly used. It's important to bear in mind that Standard English, while relatively common, is likely to be a second or even third language and will often only be used to communicate with English speakers.

You may hear Kriol spoken in Darwin. Darwin lies outside of the Kriol 'heartlands' but is nevertheless the largest town in the Northern Territory offering a wide range of employment, services and amenities not readily available elsewhere. Darwin therefore attracts many visitors and temporary residents.

As you head south down the Stuart Highway, you may turn off to the east to visit Kakadu. The name Kakadu is derived from *Gaagudju*, the name of one of the countries, languages and peoples in this region. Kriol is widely spoken here along with traditional languages.

Further south is Pine Creek which was the site of a major gold rush before the turn of the century. You will certainly hear Aboriginal people speaking Kriol around here. There's also a reasonable chance that you will hear the traditional language Mayali which has developed into a kind of lingua franca between a number of Aboriginal groups.

Continuing south, Katherine is situated close to the famous Nitmiluk (Katherine Gorge). Kriol will be one of the languages that you'll hear on the streets here.

From Katherine you can turn off the track and head southwest along the Victoria Highway which leads to the spectacular Victoria River escarpment, and over to the Kimberleys. Kriol is spoken in Aboriginal communities in the Victoria River valley region to the south of the highway, particularly by younger people and children. It's reasonably common to hear local people speaking the traditional language of Ngarinyman at Yarralin.

If continuing due south from Katherine, you might eventually be turning east onto the Central Arnhem Highway, perhaps to visit the nearby award-winning Aboriginal tourism venture, Manyallaluk. Kriol is often spoken in this southern escarpment area, being the language of everyday communication. Most members of the Aboriginal community who have grown up in these parts speak Kriol as their first language.

The next township south along the track after Katherine is Mataranka, situated near the headwaters of the Roper River and

OTHER CREOLES

famous for its thermal springs. Kriol is now the first language of almost all Aborigines in the communities here, and along the Roper Highway.

The next sizable township is Elliott. A variety of Kriol is the main language of everyday communication between Aboriginal people in Elliot but they are quick to point out that the Kriol here differs somewhat from that of the Roper area, being 'lighter' and of course being influenced by and borrowing from their traditional languages some of which are still spoken.

If we keep heading south we reach 'Three Ways' where we could turn east along the Barkly Highway if heading for Queensland. Along the Barkly Highway and to its north, including Borroloola, the everyday language of most Aboriginal people is a variety of Kriol or Aboriginal English. (In the Barkly Region it appears that Kriol may merge with Aboriginal English.)

If continuing south we arrive in Tennant Creek, which appears to be the southernmost point Kriol is spoken. This is also a 'lighter' form of Kriol. The variety of Aboriginal English which appears to be prevalent in the Barkly Region is also used. These are the everyday languages for many Aboriginal people in the town and surrounding communities. However a fair proportion of 'light' Kriol and Aboriginal English speakers still regularly use traditional 'desert' languages, most commonly Warlpiri, but also Warumungu, Warlmanpa and Mudburra.

Interacting with Kriol Speakers

The conventions used in verbal interactions among Kriol speakers follow those of traditional Aboriginal languages. What is considered appropriate or polite in conversation clearly does not always map neatly from culture to culture. Seasoned travellers will be aware of this from numerous cross-cultural experiences in other countries and they should be aware that this situation also applies in Aboriginal Australia.

Relationships

Interactions among Aboriginal people are governed by their knowledge of a complex network of family and skin name relationships. Skin names are a system for naming people according to their parentage. There are eight names – each with a male and female version – in the skin systems commonly used in the Top End and Kimberleys. These skin names categorise Aboriginal people's relationships to one another (even to people who aren't blood relatives), and thereby regulate social activities and behaviour, correct marriage partners and so on. Traditionally, an Aboriginal person won't talk to or about certain relations, such as mothers-in-law. It is considered proper for an Aboriginal person to ask for things only from certain relations, and correct form to joke around with some relations but highly inappropriate with others. Remember that as an outsider to this system there are no traditional conventions governing people's behaviour towards you. This will all depend on any individual's opportunity to learn about your culture's codes and not everyone will have had this chance.

Kriol, as with most Aboriginal languages, does not have words directly equivalent to particular English greetings, such as 'hello' goodbye' or 'good morning'. Kriol speakers with sufficient experience in English will use the relevant English greetings with non-Aboriginal people.

Greetings & Civilities

As greetings, Kriol speakers would usually call out the term designating their relationship to someone they come across, as in Dedi! 'father/dad' or Aaa, main doda! 'oh, (it's you), my daughter!' or maybe the person's skin name. Aboriginal people generally use their European-style names and their Aboriginal names less frequently than Europeans would. The use of relationship terms and skin names supplants them in most public domains.

There are also no direct equivalents of the politeness terms 'please' or 'thank you' in Kriol and other Aboriginal languages. Again, Kriol speakers familiar with the great importance that English speakers place on using such expressions will use them with non-Aboriginals. In an Aboriginal context, behaving correctly when asking or receiving something entails showing respect and a proper upbringing by having asked the correctly related person, not by using a formulaic expression.

STORI BA HANTING GADA BILIKEN[*]

Melabat bin oldei gu fishing en hanting la Hadsen Riba. Mela bin oldei wok from kemp raidap la Ol Traking Yad. Minbala main sista bin oldei kadimap ola biliken.

'Wooow!' thad olmen bin oldei faindi maidi kenggurru la fran. "Shhh!" imin laithad la melabat. 'Shhh! Jidan kwait!' imin laithad. Minbala main sista bin thad tu las pesin. Minbala bin wok gada ola biliken: *durlurl, durlurl, durlurl,* meigimbat nois laithad. 'Gudnis! Yumob dali thad dubala gel ba jidan kwait gada them biliken! Ai gada trai shuda bif ba dina!' imin laithad.

Dei bin shat: 'Yumob yangboi, dali dubala ba shadap! Kadimap ola biliken kwaitbala!' dei bin laithad. Thed lil olgumen imin jingat 'Yunbala kadimap kwaitbala them biliken! Sowunso gada shuda bif ba wi iya'.

Bat minbala bin oldei wok-w-o-o-o-k: *durlurl, durlurl, durlurl.* 'Gudnis! Nomo yumob gada bulurrum mi hanting! Yumob gada ol jidan la kemp! Yumob gada gu gada yumob matha!' imin lathed, main dedi. 'Yumob nomo bulurrumbat mi hanting! Bikos ai kan shudim eni bif wen wi faindim'. Imin laithad du.

Thad trubala, orait. Im oldei gu hanting misel thad olmen en mela ol jidan la kemp! Laik ola lil drangkinmen mela bin oldei gu hanting. Mela bin gula-gula gija olawei: Thad olmen from fran im gula la thad olgumen. Thad olgumen gula la mela da bek! En ola kenggurru bin oldei sabi wen imin irrim ola tin: *durlurl, durlurl, durlurl,* im oldei gon! No kenggurru oldei lef!

© Maureen Hodgson, 1998

Acknowledgement
Adapted from a story recorded on 15 April 1998 by Maureen Hodgson at Binjari Community near Katherine, NT, as part of the research project: A Kriol Sketch Grammar – A Description of a Modern Variety of Kriol, supported by the Australian Institute for Aboriginal & Torres Strait Islander Studies.

STORI BA HANTING GADA BILIKEN°

All of us would go fishing and hunting at Hodgson River. We would all walk from the camp right up to the Old Trucking Yard. My sister and I would carry the billycans.

'Whoooah!' our father could, say, have found a kangaroo ahead. 'Shhh!' he would say to us. 'Shhh! Be quiet!' he said. The two of us, my sister and I, were the last two people. We walked with the billycans: *rattle, rattle, rattle,* making a noise like that. 'Goodness! You lot tell those two girls to be quiet with those billycans! I've got to try and shoot some meat for dinner!' he said.

They shouted: 'You boys, tell those two to shutup! Carry the billycans quietly!' they said. The little old lady yelled 'You two carry those billycans quietly! My son-in-law (literally: 'so-and-so', an avoidance term) is going to shoot some meat for us here!'

But the two of us would keep on walking: *rattle, rattle, rattle.* 'Goodness! Never again will you lot follow me hunting! You lot are all going to stay in the camp! You lot are going to go with your mother!' my dad said, he did. 'You lot won't be following me hunting! Because I can't shoot any meat when we find it'. He said that too.

That's true alright. He would go hunting by himself that man and all of us would stop in the camp! Like little drunks we went hunting. We were telling each other off all the way: From the front our dad yelled at that old lady. That old lady would yell at us at the back! And the kangaroos would know when they heard the tins: *rattle, rattle, rattle,* they would be gone! No kangaroos would be left!

Protocol

Direct questions may be considered rude, pushy or even confrontational. In many cultures, asking questions such as someone's name, what sort of work they do and how many children they have, is considered to be showing polite interest and making your conversation partner feel at ease. This isn't the case for most Aboriginal people. A more acceptable way to start a conversation, say, if you meet up on the road somewhere, might be to offer a comment or two about your day's travel – where you've just come from or whether you found the road good or rough.

The role of silence in a conversation can be a source of significant misunderstandings between Aboriginal and non-Aboriginal people. In Aboriginal culture, silence is an entirely acceptable reaction and response. If Aboriginal people don't wish to respond verbally they are under absolutely no social or 'conversational' obligation to do so. This can be interpreted by people of other cultures as a sign of rudeness or a lack of interest, when it just means that for whatever reason the person simply feels they have no comment at this point in time.

If you were to begin a conversation with some Aboriginal people you've bumped into, they may not respond immediately, or even at all. And this is OK. Remember that an often-heard comment from blekbala 'Aboriginals' (eastern Katherine Region variety of Kriol) is that munanga or kartiya 'non-Aboriginals' (eastern and western Katherine Region varieties of Kriol respectively) talk too much and ask too many questions!

If you hold eye contact, your intentions can easily be misconstrued (maybe as threatening, aggressive or even as an indication of sexual interest) and it will almost certainly make an Aboriginal person feel uncomfortable. Conversely, if you talk to an Aboriginal person they may look in another direction. (Many non-Aboriginal people are puzzled by this at first.)

Appropriate dress is important. Non-Aboriginals waltzing up to Aboriginal people, maybe to ask directions to the shop or river, wearing their very revealing (scanty or very tight fitting) holiday garb can cause Aboriginals the greatest embarrassment. Kriol speakers approached by munanga or kartiya might studiously look in another direction hoping to avoid the impending embarrassment or they might let out exclamations of shock like Gaja!, Gardiii! or Garrrdjinga!, which in this context would mean something like 'good grief'.

Finally, there are some things that Aboriginal people just can't talk about, like sikrit bisnis, secret/sacred ceremonial matters, or people who have passed away recently. It can cause great distress and offence to speak the name of a deceased Aboriginal person within the hearing of family and community members. The same goes for showing a picture or playing an audio or video recording of someone deceased. There are many ways to avoid mentioning the name of a deceased person, for instance in referring to them by the relationship term your conversation partner would have used for them. In many places, the deceased's name goes out of currency for a period of time and anyone with the same name goes by a different one. As travellers, we won't usually know who in a community has recently passed away, so apply discretion.

On the Road

One of the most likely occasions you'll meet Kriol speakers is while on the road.

Where have you (sg/pl) come from?	Wijei yu/yumob bin kaman?
We've come from (Darwin).	Mela bin kaman brom (Darwin).
Good grief! It's a (really) long way, that is!	Gardi! Im (brabli) longwei tharran!
The road back that way, is it good/rough?	Thad rod tharrei, im gudwan/rafwan?
(I think) it's a bit/very rough.	(Ai regin) im lilbit/brabli rafwan.
No it isn't!/(No!) It's (really) good!	Najing!/Nomo! Im (brabli) gudwan!
We had a huge rain storm (back) that way.	Mela bin aba bigis rein tharrei.

OTHER CREOLES

VEHICLES	
2WD	modiga
4WD	toyoda

Did the (Victoria River) rise? — Thad (Victoria River), imin guwap?

Is the river/creek flowing? — Thad riba/krik, im raning?

We're looking for our friend/dog/car. — Mela lukaran ba mela fren/dog/modiga.

Perhaps you (sg/pl) have seen him/her/it. — Maidi yu/yumob bin luk im.

He/she has got a red car. — Im gada redwan modiga.

He/she is camping/fishing somewhere (around) here. — Im kempinat/fishing samweya iya.

He/she/it is ... — Im (gada) ...
  (rather/very) tall/long — (lilbit/brabli) longwan
  short/little — shotwan/lilwan

He/she/it has (a) ... — Im (gada) ...
  long/black hair — longwan/blekwan hey
  whiskers/beard/moustache — wiska

Directions

Which way are you (sg/pl) going? — Wijei yu/yumob gowin?

We're going ... — Mela gowin ...
  in this/that direction — dijei/tharrei
  along this/the other side of the river — disaid/najasaid la riba
  westwards/eastwards — san-gu-dan-wei/sanrais-wei
  towards Katherine — la Katherine-wei

Which direction is the river/creek/waterhole?	Wijei thad riba/krik/wodahol?
It's this/that way.	Im dijei/tharrei.
You (sg/pl) follow this road.	Yu/yumob bulurrum dis rod.

up	antap
down	ludan
ahead; in front	lida
behind; at the back	biyain
way/direction	wei

When added to the above direction terms, wei functions like adding '-ward' in English.

eastward	sanrais-wei
upward	antap-wei
foward	lida-wei
in this direction	dijei
in that direction	tharrei

Useful Phrases

It's a (very) nice spot here?	(Brabli) gudwan pleis iya.
We'd like to camp here.	Mela wandi kemp iya.
What do you (sg/pl) think?	Wani yu/yumob regin?
Is it OK?	Im rait?
We're scared of saltwater crocodiles/snakes.	Mela braitin ba eligeida/jineik.
Do you think they live here?	Yu regin im jidan iya?
Have you (sg/pl) got a/some ...?	Yu/yumob (maidi) gada ...?
lighter	laita
tobacco	dubega/sumowk
change for a phone call	sens ba ringap
spare tyre	speyawan taiya
fuel	fyuwurl
tea/sugar/food	tilib/shuga/daga

What kind of fuel do you (sg/pl) have/want?	Wotkain fyuwurl yu/yumob gadim/wandim?
Where are you/you two/you (pl) from?	Weya yu/yunbala/yumob brom?
I'm/the two of us are/we're (pl) from (overseas).	Mi/minbala/mela brom (obasis).
Where's your family?	Weya yu/yunbala/yumob femli?
They're in (Sydney).	Im la (Sydney).
My/our friends are in (Darwin).	Main/mela fren la (Darwin).
What do you (pl/sg) call this ...?	Wani yu/yumob kolim diskain ...?
fish	fish
snake	jineik
animal	enimurl
tree	tri
food	daga

INTERJECTIONS

Yuwai.	Yes.
Nomo.	No/not.
Ngabi. (also ngi or indit)	Isn't it so? (tag question)
Wanim. (also wajinim)	What's it; What's-its name. (used if you've forgotten a word)

The following have particularly high intonation (often at the end of a sentence):

gardi! (also garjinga or gaja)	good grief; oh no
bobala	poor thing/person (showing commiseration)

OTHER CREOLES

I/we call it ... in (Aboriginal) language.

Ai/mela kolim ... gada/from langgus.

Useful Words

woman (35 and older)	olguman
man (35 and older)	olmen
younger woman (15 – 30)	yanggel
younger man (15 – 30)	yangboi
girl (1 – 10)	lilgel
boy (1 – 10)	lilboi
child (1 – 10)	biginini
baby (not walking yet)	beibi
Aboriginal (eastern Katherine Region)	blekbala
Aboriginal (most of western Katherine Region)	ngumpit/ ngumbin
non-Aboriginal (eastern Katherine Region)	munanga
non-Aboriginal (western Katherine Region)	kartiya
relation(s)/family	femli
relation; family member; member of same community or language group	kantrimen

kemp

place to live/sleep. A kemp is the area in a community where people's houses are situated, someone's house (and yard), or a tarpaulin with swags if someone's camping out bush. This term isn't used just for human abodes, but also for places where animals sleep.

sweg/juweg

mattress and bedding, bedroll

demba/damba

damper (dough made with flour and baking powder which is baked in the ashes)

ejij

ashes, coals for cooking on, ash made from bark from certain trees which helps release nicotine from the tobacco with which it forms a chewing plug

graunabin

ground oven – traditional means for cooking larger animals which are placed in a hole in the ground where a fire has been lit. Meat is covered with protective material like paperbark and then covered with earth.

TOK PISIN **99**

don't just stand there, say something!

What kind of traveller are you?

A. You're eating chicken for dinner *again* because it's the only word you know.

B. When no one understands what you say, you step closer and shout louder.

C. When the barman doesn't understand your order, you point frantically at the beer.

D. You're surrounded by locals, swapping jokes, email addresses and experiences – other travellers want to borrow your phrasebook.

If you answered A, B, or C, you NEED Lonely Planet's phrasebooks.

- **Talk to everyone everywhere**
  Over 120 languages, more than any other publisher

- **The right words at the right time**
  Quick-reference colour sections, two-way dictionary, easy pronunciation, every possible subject

- **Lonely Planet Fast Talk** – essential language for short trips and weekends away

- **Lonely Planet Phrasebooks** – for every phrase you need in every language you want

'Best for curious and independent travellers' – *Wall Street Journal*

Lonely Planet Offices

Australia
90 Maribyrnong St, Footscray,
Victoria 3011
☎ 03 8379 8000
fax 03 8379 8111
email: talk2us@lonelyplanet.com.au

UK
72-82 Rosebery Ave,
London EC1R 4RW
☎ 020 7841 9000
fax 020 7841 9001
email: go@lonelyplanet.co.uk

USA
150 Linden St, Oakland,
CA 94607
☎ 510 893 8555
fax 510 893 8572
email: info@lonelyplanet.com

France
1 rue du Dahomey, 75011 Paris
☎ 01 55 25 33 00
fax 01 55 25 33 01
email: bip@lonelyplanet.fr
website: www.lonelyplanet.fr

www.lonelyplanet.com